MW00779886

SKILLUP
AS YOU
SCALEUP

THE SEVEN DIMENSIONS OF A SUCCESSFUL
STARTUP LEADERSHIP CAREER

FIRST EDITION

ADEL HAMEED

Copyright © 2024 by Adel Hameed

Book Design by Michael Trent Design
Cover Illustration © Sylverarts/Adobe Stock
Developmental Editing: Sara Kendrick
Copy Editing: Andrew Dawson
Proofreading: Erin Kelley
Marketing Copy: Rasha H. Ezzeddine

All rights reserved. No part of this publication may be reproduced, distributed, or transmitted in any form or by any means, including photocopying, recording, or other electronic or mechanical methods, without the prior written permission of the author, except in the case of brief quotations embodied in critical reviews and certain other noncommercial uses permitted by copyright law.

Paperback ISBN: 979-8-9898112-0-5
Hardback ISBN 979-8-9898112-2-9
eBook ISBN: 97:9-8-9898112-1-2

First Edition

10 9 8 7 6 5 4 3 2 1

Dedication

To my mother, my wife, and my late grandmother for always believing in me and being patient with me. To my brother, Fadel, for taking on more than his share of responsibility, freeing me up to write this book. To my kids for being an inspiration to me with their patience and positive outlook on life.

To my late dad for always challenging me to be a better person and stick to high values.

Resources

You can access the additional tools and resources mentioned throughout this book through **www.skillupasyouscaleup.com**, where I'll be diving deeper into each of the SAUS principles shared in this book. Some of the key resources you can access include:

- **SAUS infographics**

- **Training videos**

- **Links to recommended articles and books**

- **Links to all my webinars and interviews**

- **An application form to volunteer for my research projects and case studies. I'll be making the announcements through my monthly newsletters**

 Access the tools and resources by following this link
www.skillupasyouscaleup.com

Table of Contents

Acknowledgments:

I'd like to pay tribute to my mentors who enhanced my knowledge in writing this book: Ed Roberto, Dr. Samer Aljishi, Johnson Sasikumar, H.E. Khalid Alrumaihi, Dr. Nazar Al Baharna, and Dr. Simon Galpin.

Also, I'd like to thank all the following authors of referenced books and journals for permission to quote their work: Tom Kelley, Matt Blumberg, David Robson, Brad Feld, Michael Wenderoth, Jeremy Jurgens, and Stanford GSB Professors Robert Siegel, Stefanos Zenios, Ilya Strebulaev, and Jeffery Pfeffer.

Special thanks to Harvard Business Review for their support to a first-time, self-published author, and for permission to reference their diagrams and articles.

Also to publishing house Simon & Schuster and MasterClass.com for giving me permission to reference their publications.

I'm grateful to everyone who contributed their knowledge in the interviews Jad Halaoui and Abeer Nijmeh.

I'd like to thank Mike Trent for his designing efforts and acting as a partner working with me, not just another project.

Finally, my heartfelt gratitude to the CEO of PayTabs.com, Abdulaziz Aljouf, who has been a friend and a coach, allowing me to continue testing my tools to enhance the company's operations as we scale up.

Preface

Once you join as a leader, how do you know if joining a startup is the right career move for you?

If you don't find the right startup to join, is it better to wait or join one anyway?

Skill Up as You Scale Up, or as I refer to it, SAUS, is about learning as you help build a company so you can eventually reach your goals. It's a guiding philosophy that will give you the right mindset to minimize the probability of failure through incremental improvements and quick course corrections. The seven dimensions of SAUS and their principles are simple guidelines to help you be mindful of what really matters in your startup leadership role. They will help you succeed in building a scalable operation, whether you're looking after onboarding, customer care, sales, marketing, or finance.

Mastering how to manage systems is crucial for any leader working in a startup or large corporation, especially one that's outside major hubs like Silicon Valley or London. An effective and high-impact leader is responsible for designing and building a scalable function. You may have experience in the corporate world, but if you don't know how to build your operation incrementally and work with limited resources, you'll likely fail at your mission.

The reason I wrote this book is to help subject matter experts increase their chances of successfully joining growing startups as top leaders and assess whether such an environment is right for them. I connect with this because I failed many projects as a startup leader, a founder, and an investor before I got the hang of the formula and started succeeding. So I understand the pain that many go through when leaving stable jobs for the thrill (and financial rewards once things go well) of building a company. As domain experts, you could come from the corporate world, or failed startups, or maybe you were even the founder of a startup. Whatever your background, the aim of this book is to equip you with enough information to know if joining a startup is the right path for you, and if so, what is the right one to join and what is the optimal route to success. It's my mission to help others succeed in their roles as startup leaders. As we downsize in a post-COVID-19 recession at the time of writing, more startups will be formed, and they'll be responsible for creating new jobs feeding families around the world.

I saw colleagues and friends who are industry experts join startups and fail at delivering sustainable value, eventually getting terminated after a few failed projects. I had to fire some colleagues myself, which wasn't a good feeling—but I had to do what I had to do. I also saw many startup founders hire experts who lacked the team spirit and grit to succeed in a startup role. by grit, I mean having the stamina and passion to work collectively as a team, succeeding in the face of unique challenges, keeping an eye on the big picture, and not meddling in office politics.

During my journey, I had to take calculated risks which were borderline gambling, invest in startups, start my own company, and join growing startups. I had to learn through mistakes that were avoidable if I had had a book like this. Instead of thinking like a financial or business analyst, I needed to get into the weeds of the operations and understand the journey of companies like Toyota, IBM, and Apple, which grew from small enterprises to giants which have stayed at the top for decades.

I believe that achieving long-term operational excellence is a science that has been reserved for large, profitable, and well-funded—mostly manufacturing—companies. It's an area that has been neglected by most tech startups when it comes to scaling up. That's why most corporate experts fail to deliver tangible value when they join startups— because they come from an established, mature environment, and haven't gone through the pain of building an operation from scratch on limited resources trying to find an optimal tailored solution. Replicating how they worked in their previous job simply doesn't cut it. Some also fail because they don't know how to get into the weeds and learn with a fresh mindset. I'll be covering all these principles later in the seven dimensions of SAUS.

Let's assume that the startup leadership path is right for you. The next challenge is to determine whether you're looking at the right startup for you, and that it has the potential to become a profitable and successful company.

It's fascinating how companies like Google, Apple, and Spotify were able to establish scalable operational excellence as they grew that has been holding together for years. What made them different from the other startups they were competing against when they began? Google came later than Yahoo, MSN, AltaVista, Ask Jeeves, Excite, HotBot, and Lycos, but quickly surpassed them in popularity and value creation. Today, the only real competitor Google has is Microsoft's Bing due to the most recent update of ChatGPT. They all started from the seed of an idea and grew to become who they are.

Each industry is different and shaped by socio-economic, political, and technological variables. For example, companies like Microsoft and Apple had to deal with challenges such as a lack of investors who believed in them and the incumbents like IBM and Xerox who could've crushed them if they had the right people on board at the time. Airbnb had no competitors to worry about but was struggling to raise funds as it was continually rejected due to the challenges caused by its business model. Airbnb had to find a way to make it safe for hosts to rent their spare rooms to strangers and make it attractive and safe for guests to look for unique, cost-effective experiences. The ecosystem challenges keep evolving with time, and the variables also change. So it's important to be able to analyze these changes to help you assess which is the right startup for you to join that will benefit your career—and your pocket!

As time passed, Silicon Valley created a critical mass of deals that started attracting more investors, entrepreneurs, and talents until it became the global hub for tech innovation, which also had a spill-over effect on the rest of the US. However, Canve.com (from Australia) and Spotify (from Sweden) had investments from venture capitalists (VCs) in Silicon Valley that contributed to them becoming unicorns.[1] This means that you don't need to be based in Silicon Valley to become a unicorn. Studying the factors that made them global brands is fascinating, and it could also help you understand which startup is right for you to join and which to avoid.

When building and scaling a company, we start with the spirit of meri-

---

1 Unicorns refer to startups that have exceeded the valuation of $1 billion through confirmed investments by venture capital investors or through being listed on the stock market.

tocracy and open opportunity for people to rise quickly through the ranks. However, as the company grows, it becomes more challenging to keep employees away from office politics and prevent the dysfunctional behaviors that foster a lack of trust and ruin company culture over time. Protecting the agile startup culture requires understanding how scalable operational systems are built. By operational systems, I mean a combination of organizational structure, routines, and technology. Therefore, managing systems is critical to your success as a startup leader, and it will give you the mindset to thrive in the dynamics of a growing startup environment.

Robert E. Siegel, who lectures on management at Stanford and is the author of *The Brains and Brawn Company*, explains that a successful systems leader is a person who can build a customized approach between the operation of a digital and traditional system, which he compares to the anatomy of the human body. Building customized solutions that emulate the anatomy of a healthy human body requires critical and analytical thinking so you can effectively handle the challenges and opportunities of the startup, growth, and mature phases of building a company. As the company gets larger, you need to ask yourself whether you should build your capabilities internally from scratch, acquire a smaller company to build such a capability, or partner with a larger player and build on their strength. There's no one right answer to this question.

Who Is This Book For?

This book is for anyone who has an opportunity to join or has joined a growing startup (or scale up) as a senior leader, part of the top management team, or as a function owner. This book is for you if you're:

1. A corporate misfit who's fed up with the office politics which plague large companies.

2. A subject matter expert, and an entrepreneur at heart, who wants to accelerate their career.

3. A former startup founder who doesn't want to start a new startup from scratch and wants to join an existing growing startup instead.

4. A fresh university graduate who's joining a startup.

This book has a pragmatic approach toward building a successful career as a startup leader in a world that's recovering from the economic downturn triggered by the COVID-19 pandemic. I also took into account the challenges faced by developing startup hubs[2] such as Dubai (United Arab Emirates), Chennai (India), Cairo (Egypt), and Lagos (Nigeria). This book is designed to be very easy and quick to read, giving you a quick snapshot of what you need to be aware of, what you need to learn and where you can find out more about it, and how to think as a startup leader. All of this will help you increase your chances of success by avoiding the simple mistakes that most new startup leaders make.

---

2 Developing startup hubs have the foundations to support startup ecosystems, such as availability of funding, start-up-friendly regulations, and a steady flow of new startups forming and growing.

Even though most of the principles in this book can be applied in any startup ecosystem, some of the advice offered is more conservative to address the constraints in developing, rather than mature, startup ecosystems. There are already books on how to successfully navigate the startup leadership career path, such as *Startup CXO* by Matt Blumberg, which is very comprehensive and highly recommended. Reading this book will help you to absorb the information and advice in *Startup CXO*, which goes into greater detail of each function within organizations. Other books, like *Masters of Scale* by Reid Hoffman, focus on developed startup ecosystems like Silicon Valley (USA), London (UK), and Beijing (China). However, some of the advice in these books only works in developed ecosystems and could backfire if applied in emerging ecosystems. The simplest example is *Blitzscaling*, also by Hoffman (and Chris Yeh), which refers to an approach to market expansion that prioritizes speed over efficiency. For this approach to work, prerequisite conditions need to be present, which are mostly available in mature startup ecosystems. These conditions include having access to a large amount of capital and qualified investors who understand the risks and can advise how to overcome the barriers faced. It's well worth a read.

As opposed to the developed hubs I mentioned earlier, emerging startup hubs go through socio-economic changes as they evolve, with many similarities among them, making it more challenging for you to navigate through them and improve your chances of success.

How Can You Use This Book?

This book is meant to be a go-to reference as you build your operation. When you want to reflect on something you did or look for inspiration to find a solution to a challenge you're facing, skim through the principles within the applicable dimension until you find one that's relevant and it will help you move forward. Throughout the book, I'll recommend resources to help you learn more about specific subjects.

What's the SAUS Philosophy?

The SAUS philosophy is based on the belief that the quickest and most efficient way to deliver impactful results is to learn on the go instead of taking a time-out to learn a discipline or wait until you have the right resources. If you lack time, money, and skills to implement improvements, then learning through a project-oriented problem-solving approach is the ideal way to succeed in your startup leadership role. This is true specifically during the startup stage and as you scale up the operation.

As you grow into a corporation, this will change somewhere along the way. You'll be able to afford to hire specialists who will take full responsibility for implementing scalable improvements within their area of expertise. If you're in a startup, implementing full ERP (enterprise resource planning) software will be unfeasible. So, you'll end up implementing a mix of routines, spreadsheets, and Kanban boards to get the job done successfully.

This kind of pragmatic thinking requires strategic critical thinking skills that enable you to reverse engineer where you want to go in a lean manner, prioritize the projects accurately, and form your critical success path. Once you gain better clarity, you'll be more confident in your startup leadership. As you do this more often, you'll get comfortable with the approach and become faster at delivering successful implementations and positive results.

The best business schools implement a similar approach in teaching their graduate students through business case studies. In an attempt to simulate the conditions of a business case, the professors share real case studies of business problems that occurred in the past and coach their graduate students through coming up with effective solutions, then comparing them to what the companies actually did. Many of these business schools partner up with global names like General Electric, Boeing, and Microsoft to work on real projects through internships and case studies.

The challenge with implementing SAUS is that it will push you out of your conventional way of thinking and decision-making, which is usually data-driven and involves following steps and checklists with some time to breathe. However, in a growing startup environment, you have to make decisions quickly and move fast, and often, you don't have enough data to make a decision. So, the best approach is to accept the fact that you'll make mistakes. Just try to make them very small and fixable. You need to take a strategic approach to decision-making, which means factoring in data, probability, and gut feeling. Another challenge is to know when to take on the decision and responsibility alone and when to involve others.

The SAUS principles will help raise your awareness on how to overcome these challenges and become more effective at your role.

THE SAUS PHILOSOPHY WILL BENEFIT YOU BY:

1. Reducing your stress when making tough decisions.

2. Helping you effectively deliver quicker results.

3. Improving your capacity to deal with surprise situations.

4. Paving the path toward scalability through incremental improvements that stand the test of time.

5. Changing your mindset so it becomes result-driven rather than about your ego being bruised when making mistakes.

The Seven Dimensions of the SAUS Philosophy

The SAUS philosophy promotes using critical and analytical thinking to improve the accuracy of your decisions step by step and reach operational excellence as you scale up your growing startup. These incremental enhancements are achieved through implementing minimum viable optimizations (MVOs)3 to meet the business' short- to medium-term goals without consuming too many resources. I'll be elaborating more about what MVOs are in Dimension Four: Process Improvement and Optimization.

Many of us who join growing startups after many years of working in well-established corporate environments are used to working in medium to large cross-functional project teams, often up to fifty employees or more, on enhancement projects that often have long timelines. These are sometimes broken up into smaller teams, including cross-functional employees from different departments, external consultants, and employees from a corporate partner or equipment/software vendors. All decisions have to be cascaded down, and feedback has to be communicated upward to management and across the teams. It's only natural to fall back on our experience and adopt the same approach when joining a startup. However, this will most likely lead us to fail due to a lack of resources and overplanning. The belief that we'll succeed in delivering the same result if we follow the same approach is a key bias.

---

3 MVO refers to the minimum number of changes in processes or policies that are required to achieve a successful improvement in throughput, quality, or time.

From my personal experience, I was involved in an eighteen-month project implementing an enterprise resource planning (ERP) system for a medium-sized multinational enterprise that involved more than fifty cross-functional team members. The budget was more than $500,000. It ended up failing due to a lack of collaboration and accountability and, later, funding. So I learned a lot from it, which enabled me to avoid the same mistakes that were made in that project. Many years later, I had to lead the implementation of a customer support ticketing system within a startup environment with a project team of five people and a budget of only $1,000. I had to look at it with a fresh mindset, following what I call the MVO approach, which helped me focus on the critical path to success and leave every other require-ment for later. Yes, it worked. Within one year, we went from having daily complaints to being one of the top-rated payment companies in the MENA region.

When solving problems at a startup, you don't have the time, money, or staff to pause things, learn, or hire consultants to solve the problem for you. You have to learn by adopting a problem-solving mindset where you outline the goal, how you can achieve the goal, and what the deliverables are.

You must be intentional as you build the components of your company with the bigger picture in mind. Like laying the foundations of a house, you need to develop the blueprint design, then gradually build each room and floor as needed while giving yourself the flexibility to adjust your blueprint as you pivot and discover new constraints.

Aiming at perfection or avoiding failure is unrealistic and counterproductive because it leads to overplanning, overanalyzing, and expensive delays, which could result in losing your job and possibly bankrupting the startup. The SAUS principles are built to help you become a better and more confident decision-maker and learn what you need to succeed.

What Is a Scale-up?

A scale-up is a growing startup that has achieved significant success in the startup phase and is ready for the next level. They have created a name for themselves in a city or a country with one or two products and are experiencing rapid growth and expansion. With a proven business model, a steady revenue stream, and a growing customer base, tech startups must expand their market share beyond their state or country. So if the startup was formed in Delhi and they achieved success in Delhi, they need to start expanding into the rest of India and beyond, which requires cash injection from investors instead of focusing on profitability. Scale-ups require capital injection for every country they expand into or for any product they launch, although they differ in profitability when they achieve a level of maturity. So, they mostly continue to face funding limitations and operational efficiency challenges as they strive to sustain their growth trajectory. The company's growth stage is one of the key factors that will impact your decision on whether to join, stay, or leave.

The term startup has been used for decades, but the term scale-up has recently surfaced to describe growing startups that are focused on expanding market shares to dominate regions or continents. It has become a popular term in publications in recent years, although most investors don't typically use it to represent a stage of maturity. Instead, they look at the evolution of a startup by funding stages such as pre-seed, seed, startup, series A, series B, and series C. Most investors aim for a rewarding exit that will enable them to sell their shares for a return in multiples of the amount they invested at the beginning, as opposed to low-risk investments, which typically return up to 7% annually in the best economic conditions.

What is a Scale-Up?

Scale-Up Journey

	Preseed	Seed	Series A	Series B	Series C	Series D+	Public Offering
Growth Rate							
Fund Raised	$50,000 to $500,000 (Sometimes up to $1 Million)	$100,000 to $6 Million	$5 to $20 Million	$10 to $50 Million	$30 to $500 Million	$100+	$100+
Average Period from Start	3 to 9 Months	12 to 18 Months	12 to 36 Months	24 Months	51 Months (27 Months B to C)	+60 Months	+60 Months
Valuation (Pre-Money)		$3 to $6 Million	Up to $24 Million	$40 to $60 Million	$100 to $200 Million		
Number of Staff	Founders (Sometimes a couple of employees)	2 to 10 People (Sometimes only the founders)	10 to 110 Employees	90 to 280 Employees	200 to 1000	Going from 100's to 1000's	Going from 100's to 1000's
Locations	One	One	Small Region	Large Region	Global	Global	Global
Typical Investors	Founders (Friends & Family) and Small Investors	Accelerators and some VC's	VC and some Angel Investors	VC	VC	VC	VC (+ Public Shareholders in the case of IPO)
Purpose	Ensure the idea is viable and is worth investing resources into a pitch and a prototype.	Product-Market-Fit through developing a Minimum-Viable-Product and many iterations.	Build a revenue-generating and working product. Create a scalable blueprint.	Identified Product-Market-Fit. Capture as many customers as possible while establishing operational efficiency and scalability. Path to profitability.	Build a new product and expand into new markets.	They have lowered the risk of the startup, and they have proved that they're scaling and need to accelerate the scaling globally.	Alternatively, they want to reward their investors with an exit and to scale globally.

Disclaimer: These numbers are still work-in-progress and are only used to educate the audience on the thinking process and the abstract logic behind the rounds that lead to scaling up a company.

Figure 1: The scale-up journey

"Startups are a catalyst for economic growth both globally and locally. The value that startups create is nearly on par with the GDP of a G7 economy and the amount of startup funding in 2021 surpassed $600 billion, shattering funding records. The number of unicorns is well past the 1,000 mark and growing exponentially."[4]

Jeremy Jurgens,
Managing Director,
World Economic Forum

4 Jeremy Jurgens, "How Startups Drive Economic Recovery While Growing Responsibly," *World Economic Forum*, May 12, 2022, https://www.weforum.org/agenda/2022/05/how-startups-help-drive-economic-recovery-and-growth.

Many experts and economists consider startups to be critical drivers of economic growth and innovation, as they create jobs, enhance the quality of services offered to citizens, and contribute to the overall vitality of the business ecosystem.

The Importance of Scalability

Regardless of your industry, marketplace, or mission, the stages a company goes through to become an established corporation are all the same. A corporation or enterprise is a profit-making company that is either listed on a public stock exchange or a privately owned shareholding company.

Before a company becomes a listed corporation, it must earn its stripes to be defined as a corporation. It must have expanded in its target region with an evolving mix of products and a clear, competitive position in the market. It needs to have high margins and steady growth toward profitability, if not already profitable.

By the end of the scale-up phase, your company's stock should be so attractive that, once the company goes public through an initial public offering (IPO), investors will flock to buy your shares, and the set price of the share will keep rising. That is the ideal scenario.

To get there, a company has to build a scalable operation that has business continuity, efficiency, and excellence embedded within its DNA. The following four components are some of the building blocks of a scalable operation:

1. TRANSPARENT PROCESSES

Transparent processes that every employee in every department quickly understands. That means if someone gets hit by a bus or wins the lottery and leaves, someone else can continue following the same process with minimal service delivery disruption.

2. CLEAR ORGANIZATIONAL STRUCTURE

Clear organizational structure with each function's role within each service's value creation flow outlined. This includes establishing strategic tools and methods such as key performance indicators (KPIs); objectives and key results (OKRs); and responsible, account-able, consulted, and informed (RACI) matrices for projects.

The **OKRs** of the company and all its functions should align with those of the CEO. For example, if one of the deliverables is to be rated as 4.5 out of 5 on Google Reviews or Trust Pilot, then who is account-able for this, and how will it be cascaded? It would probably look something like the figure below.

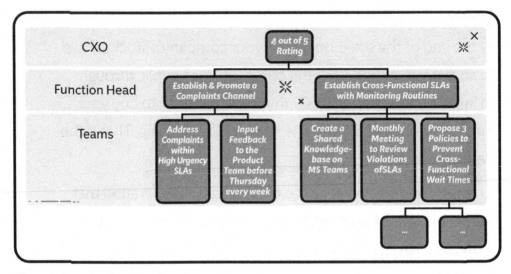

Figure 2: Owners of company functions

KPIs are metrics that will help you assess your current position and where you're heading in the future. Some examples include:

- **Customer Acquisition Cost**: This represents the cost to acquire and obtain one active customer or a customer that makes a purchase. The definition of an active customer might vary based on your business model. If you're model is a software subscription—Software-as-a-Service (SaaS)—business model, then the qualifying criterion would be any customer who paid for at least one month's subscription. If it's a campaign you're running for your existing customers to upgrade, then the criteria will be narrower. This could be through upselling to a premium version or cross-selling related products to enhance their experience.

$$Customer\ Acquisition\ Cost\ (CAC) = \frac{Sales\ and\ Marketing\ Expenses}{Number\ of\ New\ Customers}$$

This KPI aims to measure your campaigns' performance, compare with previous ones, and benchmark against industry standards. This will also help you justify customer retention incentives when compared against the customer churn and customer lifetime value (LTV).

- **Customer Conversion Rate**: This is a percentage of potential customers you convert into paying customers. Depending on the business model, the definition of converted customer might change.

For example, if you're an online retail store, then you could define a customer as someone who has made a purchase, and put a heavier emphasis on revenue per visitor (RPV) and average order value (AOV).

$$Conversion\ Rate\ (\%) = \frac{Number\ of\ Purchases}{Number\ of\ Visitors} x\ 100$$

If you have a SaaS[5] business model and are subscription-based, then the formula will be as follows:

$$Conversion\,Rate\,(\%) = \frac{Number\,of\,New\,Customers}{Number\,of\,Leads} x\,100$$

In the SaaS model, you'll need to narrow the focus on the types of customer that add the highest value to your business so you can double-down on servicing them, whether they're large-volume low-margin customers or low-volume high-margin customers. Measuring the monthly recurring revenue (MRR), customer acquisition cost (CAC), and customer lifetime value (LTV) will help you better understand who you need to focus on and how long it takes to convert existing customers into paying ones, referred to as the sales cycle length. The usual hypothesis is, the shorter the conversion and onboarding cycle, the higher the conversion rate, and the lower the cost. However, achieving that usually entails overcoming many internal and external challenges.

- **Operating Profit**: This is an excellent KPI to measure the health of the business and how far your startup is from profitability.

$$Operating\,Profit = Gross\,Profit - Operating\,Expenses - Depreciation - Amortization$$

It usually takes a startup three to four years to turn an operating profit. If it's a tech startup, then it might take even longer as the need to gain regional or global market share trumps the need to achieve immediate profitability. If developing the technology is too expensive to serve

---

5 Software-as-a-Service (SaaS) is a model offered by many software providers, such as Microsoft, Adobe, and Google, where a customer pays a monthly or annual subscription to use the software.

just one country or a small population, then gaining a larger market share is crucial. Also, introducing services and features that offer more value to the customers and better margins for your startup will help you get closer to achieving a positive operating profit.

This is a moving target. You always have to keep an eye on it as you respond to market and business model changes.

You can find more examples of KPIs in the Resources section.

The **RACI matrix** or chart, whether it's written as a table or not, details the function head responsible for a specific area, who will be accountable for the result of each task, whose expertise or feedback is needed, and who will be impacted and needs to be informed. This way, you ensure clarity of communication and coordination with all stakeholders, which is necessary for the success and stickiness of any project. The following is an example of a RACI matrix for a campaign to launch a new product.

DELIVERABLES	RESPONSIBLE	ACCOUNTABLE	CONSULT	INFORM
Write the Plan	Marketing Manager	Marketing Manager Commercial Manager	Product Head Country General Manager	Product Head Country General Manager
Ads Design	Graphic Designer	Marketing Manager Commercial Manager	Product Head Country General Manager	Product Head Country General Manager
Web Page Design	Web Designer	Marketing Manager Commercial Manager	Product Head Country General Manager	Product Head Country General Manager
Launch the Campaign	Marketing Officer	Marketing Manager Commercial Manager	Product Head Country General Manager	Product Head Country General Manager

Figure 3: RACI matrix for launch of a new product campaign

3. FUNDING RUNWAY

Startups focus on increasing their cash runway by reducing their burn rate so the money lasts longer. One way to do this is by compensating employees, including leaders, with employee stock ownership plans (ESOPs). So, it's important to know the rules of the shares and the major rounds of fundraising to determine the likely success of the company continuing to raise bridge funding. This is important because your shares will be worth nothing if the company shuts down. All you'll have are some bruises from the experience and a salient lesson to take into your next similar or higher role at a startup or in the corporate world.

The ESOPs help founders attract and retain the best talent out there while saving on the salaries and benefits that the corporate world offers. They also give employees a vested interest in the success of the company, ensuring they direct their entrepreneurial spirit and blood, sweat, and tears toward making it work (thereby increasing the value of their shares).

Let's assume that you're working as a marketing manager for an established hotel chain and earn $5,000 a month with additional benefits, such as an annual bonus of up to a third of your salary, a phone and car allowance, excellent health and life insurance, and an education allowance for your kids. A holiday marketplace startup approaches you to join them as CXO of marketing. They have been operating for two to three years and have raised around $10 million in funding. They're working on raising more in the next round to scale up the operation, and the CEO expects you to build a mature operation that supports the company's expansion plan. However, most likely, the company won't be able to offer you the same as your current package. Instead, they'll offer less or the same salary but compensate you with shares that will be vested over four years. You only start to receive your shares upon completing your first year, after which you earn the rest on a pro-rata basis. This is referred to as four-year vesting with a one-year cliff.

4. A STRONG LEADERSHIP TEAM

A strong leadership team that work harmoniously and act as partners, not just employees. When a startup starts growing from the seed stage, the team are generally less experienced and learn as they go. Here, the leaders are more generalists than specialists. As the startup grows, so does the need for specialists. This means that responsibilities will be taken away from the earlier leaders or function owners. This can cause resentment, especially if the previous leaders have to report to the new specialist.

Let's illustrate this with an example. Sanjeev is the CXO responsible for sales and business development. Ankita then joins as the CXO responsible for business development. Sanjeev is a bit peeved as he feels this undermines his position. He also worries that Ankita has been hired because he's been underperforming. So Sanjeev might sabotage the handover and lobby against Ankita, who will have to work extra hard to make sure she gains some allies and delivers results quickly. Otherwise, she could lose her job. Sanjeev is using the same Machiavellian politics commonplace in his previous roles in the corporate world to scupper Ankita's work, putting the company's progress at risk because he's lost perspective of what really matters. Imagine if you are Ankita.

People like Sanjeev hate employees having the power to make decisions themselves. They jealously guard their knowledge in the belief it will make them indispensable and prove their value and influence to everyone, even if it causes a bottleneck in the flow of information across the company.

This is an important aspect to look for when assessing a company before making a commitment or taking a serious step. You need to look for signs of dysfunction when you go through the interviewing process and meet other CXOs and function heads.

The list could go on, but I'll focus on these four critical components for now.

Finally, before becoming a startup, much less a scale-up, you need to have a product or a service that has been proven under test conditions. For example, proving demand via a sample group of your target customers showing willingness to pay through existing sales or a signed letter of intent (LOI).[6] This is known as the "seed" stage. If you only have an idea but not a product, the stage will be called "pre-seed."

The meanings may vary among the stages I mentioned above, but the concept on an abstract level is the same.

It's important that your company is prepared for the scale-up phase, where more funding pours in so you can continue expanding and capturing market share as fast as possible. In this stage, cash burns quickly, and if you get into it before you've considered the scalability of your company, it could backfire. You can easily burn your company's

---

6 In the startup world, a letter of intent is used as an expression of interest from an existing or potential customer in purchasing products once they are available on the market.

brand and lose the trust of your investors by wasting their time and money. If that happens, you will likely spiral into bankruptcy.

There are always exceptions to this scenario, typically in Silicon Valley, but the environment is less tolerant in regions like the Middle East, Africa, and Central Asia. Your company could be sucked into a hostile takeover by a corporation where it's sold to the highest bidder against the will of the founders.

The Risks of Dreaming about Unicorns

Rarely have I met a founder who does not dream of their company becoming a unicorn and tries to convince everyone around them that it's going to happen. This is especially true with first-time and younger entrepreneurs. I always asked myself, *How come they're so sure? Why are they trying so hard to convince themselves and everyone around them? Is it a sign of being delusional? Does this mean that they'll do anything to achieve that, regardless of morals or ethics? If I join them, will I have to deal with the conflicting egos of several founders who see each other as equals because they haven't appointed one as CEO?* These are just some of the many questions that I needed to consider before deciding to join a specific startup and lock myself into a company for at least the next five years.

As you get older and more experienced, you probably have more personal responsibilities and financial commitments. Therefore, the stakes are higher if you lose your job or the startup goes bankrupt. The last thing you want to do is waste your time and energy on a startup that you think will flop or inflict unnecessary pain due to its dysfunctional culture.

You could lose money, damage your reputation, waste your time, and potentially suffer burnout. All you can do to mitigate these risks is understand the factors that enable you to take a calculated guess before you join. But there are no guarantees—sometimes you just have to take a leap of faith and put all your effort and energy into making it work.

Your reward for that risk will be an employee stock ownership plan (ESOP). These are shares that you earn, usually over four years, with a cliff at the end of the first year. For example, 25% of your shares are given to you once you finish one year, and then the rest you'll earn on a monthly basis. This condition protects the other shareholders from having employees with ESOPs who don't contribute to the business. You can consider the first-year cliff as a probation period for the shares. The earlier you join the startup, the higher the risk so the more shares you earn. To learn more about this subject, I recommend you read the book *Venture Deals* by Brad Feld and Jason Mendelson.[7] Visit the resources website of this book for a link to their cohort-based course.

There are lots of excellent books, podcasts, and articles on scale-ups. You can find recommendations by visiting my resources website. However, you have to keep in mind that many of these stories are of unicorns based in developed startup ecosystems. Most of these authors overlook the conditions in the startup ecosystems of developing economies.

According to a LinkedIn post by Stanford professor Ilya Strebulaev, only 27% of 2,321 unicorn founders graduated from universities outside the US.[8] When you look at the graph on the next page (Figure 4), you see that those universities are limited to six countries only. Theoretically, this means if you're joining a startup where none of the founders are graduates of these universities, the chances are slim that it will become a unicorn. However, I expect this will change, and there will be more universities producing unicorn leaders in the US and globally in the future.

---

7 Brad Feld and Jason Mendelson, *Venture Deals: Be Smarter than Your Lawyer* and *Venture Capitalist*, Fourth edition (Hoboken, New Jersey: Wiley, 2019).

8 Professor Ilya Strebulaev, Stanford GSB, LinkedIn post, May 2022, https://www. linkedin.com/posts/ilyavcandpe_ unicorns-startups-university-activity-6932340877449191424-1wa0.

As part of your assessment process of the startup you're considering joining, you have to factor in that many of the successful unicorn founders we know today have been university dropouts. These founders include Elon Musk, founder of Space X; Bill Gates, founder of Microsoft; and Reid Hoffman and Peter Thiel, founders of PayPal. Some of these founders were terrible in school and university. So, if the founders of the startup you're joining or working for already, are not a graduates of major universities or are dropouts, then it doesn't mean that they won't be unicorn material because there are other factors you need to consider such market demand for your service or product, competition in the market, competitive position in the market, or the founder's superpowers and their access to special resources. By super-powers, I refer to their special skills such as fundraising and their skill in hiring great leaders.

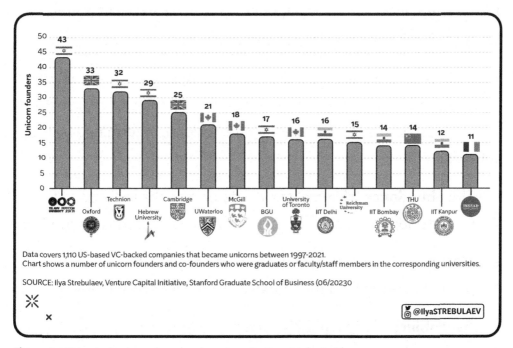

Data covers 1,110 US-based VC-backed companies that became unicorns between 1997-2021.
Chart shows a number of unicorn founders and co-founders who were graduates or faculty/staff members in the corresponding universities.

SOURCE: Ilya Strebulaev, Venture Capital Initiative, Stanford Graduate School of Business (06/20230

@IlyaSTREBULAEV

Figure 4: US-backed unicorn founders by university they graduated from

Many founders will keep telling you that their companies will become unicorns, and it may be a justifiable ambition, but you have to take it with a pinch of salt. Becoming a unicorn isn't the only good outcome there. Another rewarding outcome for all shareholders could be an acquisition by larger player because you'll all be able to sell some of the shares you own in the startup for large sums, usually multiples of the value when you earned them. There are companies, such as Rocket Internet, whose business model is based on replicating successful US companies and selling these startups to unicorns in the US, making large profits in the process.

However, it's important to understand that without a successful exit through mergers and acquisitions (M&A) or an initial public offering (IPO), your earned shares have no value. Once you join, you have to remain focused on delivering value by establishing a scalable operation that will help you get closer to a successful exit. Success rates should improve as we get out of the global economic uncertainty post-COVID-19.

In addition to your ability to build a scalable operation, there are other variables that contribute to increasing the probability of your success. Location of the startup is a major factor, which is determined by the following:

- **The abundance of investors** will determine the likelihood of raising bridge funding and closing on upcoming funding rounds.

- **Maturity of the investment laws and regulations**, which protects the rights of the founders, investors, and employees.

- **Availability of high quality talent** through the universities based in that ecosystem.

- **Size of the market** and access to other markets through economic agreements.

- **Cost of living and operating a business**; the lower it is, the more attractive it is for startup founders and students.

- **Availability of financial incentives** such as financial grants or tax breaks.

Silicon Valley has positioned itself as a springboard for startups to scale up their operations and dominate the global markets. When a startup in one of the international startup ecosystems has proven its readiness to expand, it means that they're ready to move to Silicon Valley and scale in the US and then globally. So what makes Silicon Valley so unique?

To better understand the evolution of startup ecosystems, we'll look at it through an economic development lens. The table on the next page aims to give you an idea of how startup ecosystems evolve in emerging, developing, and developed economies. This will help you assess the potential for success and growth of the startup you're looking to join as a leader.

	Emerging	Developing	Developed
Traction	Low	Medium	High
Income Per Capita	$100-$2,000	$2,000 to $10,000	More than $10,000
Transportation Infrastrcuture	Distance reached in one hour = 10-20 kilometers (6-12 miles) Tight roads, some unpaved. Travel between the village and a city on a bicycle.	Distance reached in one hour = 20-50 kilometers (12-31 miles) Basic highways, business streets. Lots of traffic lights limited direct flights.	Distance reached in one hour = 50-100 kilometers (31-62 miles) High speed trains connecting cities, highways connecting cities.
Capital Markets	Low liquidity, basic regulations, high transaction costs, no IPO insfrastrcuture.	Basic access to financial instruments, developing financial regulations, available market data, increased number of digital financial services, and available local public stock market.	High liquidity in the market and attractive for regional and global investors. Mature regulatory framework protecting investors. Clear track towards IPO regionally or globally.
ICT Infrastructure	All paper-based government transactions, expensive and basic access to the internet, and limited access to open-data.	Access to high-speed internet at a competitive price. Increasing adoption of smartphones. increasing audience for locally created content, entreprenuers work from coffeeshops.	+99% smartphone adoption, connection of low-cost fiber optic nationwide, coworking spaces abundantly available, locally available datacenters.
Cultural Diversity	Less open to global visitors, strict labor laws prohibit expats from moving in and working locally, employer has the upper hand over expat employee movement.	Promoting inward investment for foreign investors, setting up startup ecosystems, introducing regulations that protects investors and entreprenuers against personal liabilities, offers grants for innovation (No major startups that went to global IPO or became Unicorns.)	Attractive immigration policies, IPO success stories, top universities feeding into the startup ecosystems.
Education Infrastructure	Low quality underfunded universities with limited options for local workforce.	A mix of public and private universities and technical schools with varying levels of quality controls.	Available business schools that collaborate with the private sector. Ivy league schools.
Startup Friendly government policies	Lowering levels of corruption through government initiatives and started to digitize services online.	Improved transparency through egovernment services and transparent service delivery timeilness.	All government services are on continuous improvements and all government services are online and transparent. Business arbitration and dispute resolution is fast.
Tolerance to founder failures	Low	Medium	High
Examples	Riyadh, Bahrain, Manila, Casablanca, and Accra	Istanbul, Jakarta, Dubai, Seoul, and Singapore	Silicon Valley, London, Berlin, Banglore, Beijing

Figure 5: Characteristics of emerging, developing and developed economies

The US produces more than 48% of unicorns globally (Figure 6).[9] From there, they can launch an IPO on the US stock exchanges. If the founders are not based in the US, and they want to launch a startup based in Silicon Valley, they have to take one of the following routes:

- Launch their startup through incubators and accelerators;

- Launch their startup immediately after graduating from a US university;

- Start in their home country and grow into their region, then apply for an acceleration program in Silicon Valley-based accelerators and incubators; or

- Get lucky with a Silicon Valley-based venture capital (VC) investment company.

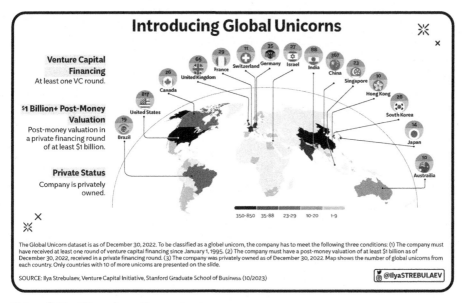

Figure 6: The US produces the most unicorns

9 Ilya Strebulaev, "Contribution of Global Unicorns by Ilya Strebulaev. Jpeg," October 19, 2023, https://www.linkedin.com/posts/ilyavcandpe_venturecapital-unicorns-activity-712 0791856304508930-0rYg?utm_source=share&utm_medium=member_desktop.

There are other routes to take that are less obvious, but these are the most common ones. Some governments create soft-landing zones in Silicon Valley for their home-grown startups and run programs that funnel only the best startups into Silicon Valley. I've seen these landing zones inside existing Silicon Valley incubators and accelerators. If a VC in your region has invested in your startup, they most likely have the partnerships needed to help you move into Silicon Valley and successfully raise the funding needed to expand globally. However, these cases are very rare for startups coming out of developing startup ecosystems.

How Does the Ecosystem Maturity Impact Your Startup Leadership Career?

As a startup leader in Silicon Valley, you would have to compete with top talent from Ivy League universities. Theoretically, you have a better chance of becoming successful in developing markets due to less competition in the job marketplace.

However, this also means that when you hire people, it will be difficult to attract the top talent, especially with your limited budget. You will keep facing points where you need to slow your cash burn rate due to delays in funding—presenting challenges in retaining or attracting the best people—recruitment freezes, product launch delays, expansion delays, and much more. You will have to think strategically and be mentally and tactically prepared while minimizing any damage a failed experiment or innovative project could cause.

In many emerging markets, unlike Silicon Valley, bankruptcy law is not as lenient toward startup failures, meaning founders and investors could be liable for the losses. A lack of cash caused by customers not paying invoices on time, for example, could suck the company into a black hole. Bills keep piling up, employees do not get paid their salaries on time—let alone receiving bonuses or raises—and founders take personal loans to keep the company afloat. There is often a collective cognitive bias by founders and their employees similar to Stockholm Syndrome[10] – believing claims like, "We're almost there." This takes

---

10 Stockhom Syndrome is a psychological phenomenon where the victim of a kidnapping starts to sympathize with their captors and defend them.

place when employees keep empathizing with the founders' false claims at the expense of their own future and beliefs they have. It is a bad situation to be in.

In Silicon Valley, investors and founders are not personally liable for their company's debts when facing bankruptcy. However, they may lose their investment in the company if it goes bankrupt. This freedom from long-term and personal liabilities allows them to fail early and not pull themselves, the investors, and the employees into a delusional web of lies.

In exchange for this freedom, the regulations in Silicon Valley require companies to declare bankruptcy if they reach a point where they cannot pay their debts, including the salaries of employees, rather than delaying them, which is common in many emerging ecosystems.

Finally, you need to be aware of the difference in ESOPs. In Silicon Valley, the mechanism is transparent and well-recognized by employers, regulators, employees, and the rest of the ecosystem. However, in most emerging markets, it is not. The founders make promises, but they shy away from them. Many of them go back on their word and delay the process.

Most regulators have these issues on their radars and aim to implement regulations to overcome such challenges, but many are slow to do so. Most governments in emerging regions are becoming more aware of the need to build a startup ecosystem to close a gap with developed startup ecosystems and differentiate themselves from the rest of the world. To create ecosystems, many regulatory changes and promotion of investment is needed. This will build investors' trust, attract regional talents as founders and employees, and create a sand-box environment for startups to test their products and scale into the local market. It also means ESOPs are recognized by local regulators even if the employer issued them in a tax haven such as the Cayman Islands or Singapore.

Navigating through the Hard Times

While I have been writing this book, the global economy has been impacted heavily by the rising global debt ceiling due to COVID-19. It became more expensive for emerging economies to get loans due to the high risk of nonrepayment. Countries had to invest in vaccines, provide unemployment benefits to their citizens, and recover from trade disruptions they faced during the peak of the spread of the virus. The US government started increasing the interest rate to control inflation, which has a global cascading effect. The oil and gas supply shortages are another contributor, causing power cuts in many countries.

The ripple effect of these events on local economies meant everyone was impacted. There are additional intermediate pressures, such as a rise in the cost of living, a drop in purchasing power, and drop in the average household income. As a result, the market for many products keeps shrinking, which means fewer people are needed to manufac-ture and sell products or support customers.

In addition, the dramatic rise in the use of artificial intelligence (AI) and robotic process automation (RPA) to replace mundane basic jobs is contributing further to loss of employment—and the resulting social unrest.

Such ebbs and flows are a normal part of the economic cycle. The good news is that some people who lose their jobs will start companies, creating new jobs and bringing purchasing power back to the economy. Only time will tell if we will return to the prosperity we had before COVID-19 struck.

In late 2022, some experts predicted that a new wave of startups would be created, and VCs would start focusing on early-stage startups. I am not a finance expert, but this makes sense because investors can pick and choose from so many new ideas and startups. To take advantage of this emerging trend, you need to know which startup to join, how to succeed at your role, and how to work with the founders and your colleagues to hit the necessary milestones when scaling the company.

Why Are the SAUS Principles Different from Everything Else Out There?

The SAUS principles are unique for the following reasons:

1. They focus on startup leaders who are employees, not cofounders. Most other startup books are written for founders and entrepreneurs.

2. They are designed for busy people; simple and short.

3. They reference the best resources to learn more about a specific principle.

4. They are aimed at corporate misfits and dropouts who want to do more with their careers.

5. They are a more pragmatic approach than most startup career advice books.

I built the SAUS principles to help you succeed in your new startup leadership role during these challenging times. These principles were forged from the pain of my own experiences of trying different solutions to a myriad of challenges and the lessons I learned from the collective wisdom of mentors, colleagues, peers, and authors.

To keep things short, I didn't include case studies or go into too much depth. However, I will share these stories in my newsletters, webinars, videos, and in future books as part of the SAUS series. It is my mission to give you the knowledge you need to succeed in your new role while remaining motivated. No one wants to follow an indecisive leader, so it's the beginning of the end if you start doubting yourself just because you made a couple of mistakes.

Think of this book as the compass which guides you on the startup leadership career path. The SAUS principles will keep you on track so you avoid the common pitfalls that most executives fall into, whether you are from a corporate background or have been promoted internally through the ranks. This advice will help you recalibrate your thinking to be that of a business partner rather than employee. In the corporate world, we tend to submit to authority and respect boundaries, most of the time at the expense of the collective success of the organization.

Finally, the SAUS principles apply, to various degrees, to leadership roles in any department of the startup, whether it's finance, operations, or compliance. Each principle is part of a bigger concept that will help you think more deeply and strategically, all while remaining mindful of the critical factors which will help your organization successfully achieve its business objectives and help you become a great leader.

It Is Important to Think as a Partner, Not an Employee

The default thinking of experts who spend their career in a multi-national corporation is they are an employee, not a partner. Some might argue that to think otherwise when you don't own shares in the company is delusional. But this approach can blind us to essential factors for a successful startup. It is counter to the way that CEOs and board members assess our performance in a startup environment.

Also, you are probably reporting to the CEO or the COO and have to respond whenever you are called upon for a special project or to support an initiative. You also have to work closely with your peers and understand how their functions fit in the overall structure, especially from a value creation and delivery perspective.

For example, a chief financial officer (CFO) who thinks as a partner will focus on value creation, growth, and efficiency instead of building influence through being a controlling gatekeeper of the cash. There are other examples that I will be showcasing in the SAUS series videos, articles, and books.

> *"Many founders make the mistake of hiring a whole team of generalists who are like the founders in skills and tendencies. Later, we discover that we need a mix of generalists and specialists to ensure the company grows and scales successfully."*
>
> Jad Halaoui, cofounder and
> COO of Washmen.com

How SAUS Will Help You Succeed as a Leader

When I interviewed Jad Halaoui, COO and cofounder of Washmen. com, he confirmed that scaling up an operation requires a leadership team that consists of both specialists from the corporate world with a core area of expertise and generalists with diverse experience spread over two to three areas that can fill any role. He also added that, like many startups, he and his cofounders had to fire leaders who avoided getting into the details of the operation to understand the root cause of the challenges they were facing.

It's challenging, prior to hiring these leaders, to assess whether they will fit the culture and have a systems design mindset or not. Many CEOs contribute to the failure of these seasoned leaders by not questioning their understanding of the constraints they have to deal with to establish a scalable operation. Most of these startup leaders come from a middle management job in a corporation, so they have limited training in becoming more effective strategic thinkers. As for the leaders that come from a corporate C-level position, they lack the readiness to get into the weeds of the operation, which also leads them to fail as they are disconnected from the reality on the ground.

So, there are two angles here: the first is you as the person joining the startup as a leader; and the second is you hiring someone as part of your team as you scale up the operation. In the first angle, whether you're coming from middle management or from a C-level position in a corporation, you need to understand the pitfalls to avoid and the factors for success if you are going to find your groove and grow. In the second angle, when hiring someone, it's important to assess their expectation and their personality before getting them to leave a secure job and join you. Cutting corners in this situation could cause you lots of delays in the long run. I can think of a few people whom I worked with in my previous roles who, despite their experience and charisma, turned out to be toxic personalities that were politically savvy enough to fog outcomes and dodge bullets by shifting blame to others.

The seven dimensions and their principles will enable you, as a startup leader, to find the right startup to join, build a strong culture, and avoid pitfalls and biases. This will help you earn the trust of the CEO and the rest of your colleagues and be seen as a partner and a capable leader instead of only an employee on the payroll.

There are seventy-five principles broken down into seven dimensions. Each dimension will help you implement a critical routine or avoid a pitfall, which will eventually lead to success in your role. I've included recommended references to learn more. I'll keep updating these on the accompanying references website.

The SAUS principles will help you be more intentional and proactive with your work and decisions, so there are fewer surprises and you are comfortable dealing with them when they arise. They'll give you a framework to organize your thoughts and give you greater mental clarity so you can quickly spot what matters, ask the right questions as you solve problems, and prioritize more effectively. Each dimension will help you calibrate your thinking to that of your new role as a startup leader. This will help you become more focused as you deliver results that contribute to the startup's success and will be much appreciated by the CEO and your colleagues. This will enable you to foster a positive culture as you build and scale the company's operation.

Think of these seven dimensions as lenses. The view through each will give you something to focus on. They are as follows:

I. **Dimension One: Self-control and Leadership.** Build habits that will make you a more effective and collected startup leader throughout the scaling journey.

II. **Dimension Two: Customer Centricity.** Focus all cross-departmental activities, and the rationale behind all decisions, on the customer's experience.

III. **Dimension Three: Culture and Team.** Make bold decisions to ensure a culture of growth and operational excellence which attracts and retains the best talent.

IV. **Dimension Four: Process Improvement and Optimization.** Scope and deliver initiatives and projects to improve incrementally as part of a roadmap, not just for short-term wins.

V. **Dimension Five: Founders.** Manage your relationship with the founders and focus on the objective and value delivery.

VI. **Dimension Six: Investors.** Identify what investors and board members need to be effective, both in their roles and in supporting the CEO. Communicate effectively to align the board with the CEO and the activities of the startup as a whole.

VII. **Dimension Seven: Community.** Ensure your work benefits your local community while also serving your objectives.

How to Get the Best Out of This Book

This book aggregates my experiences and those of other startup leaders I know. No doubt there will be more to come as more startup leaders join different industries in different regions. To get the most out of this book, I recommend reading it once to familiarize yourself with the concepts, then keep referring to it when you feel lost or want to reflect.

This book is written to be light and easy to digest. That's why I left out lots of details that will be available through the website and the upcoming books I'm working on. I'll keep sharing related articles and videos through my channels. You can scan the QR code, which is also available in the Resources section at the end of this book. Make sure you sign up to stay up to date.

Dimension One:

Self-Control and Leadership

Before you can gain objective control over your team and move projects forward, you must gain control over yourself. You need to build habits and routines that will help you avoid distractions and stay focused on what matters and deliver the most value to your organization, whether you are diving into the weeds of problems or zooming out to a helicopter view. So, how can you do this? The following principles will make you a better leader.

1. **Personal productivity and organization are critical to your success**. The fastest and most reliable way to be more productive is to manage your thoughts and wisdom in a way that frees your mind to focus on what matters. I combined David Allen's Getting Things Done (GTD) and Tiago Forte's Building a Second Brain (BASB) methods, detailed in their books of the same names. The GTD method helped me process tasks by dividing them into up to three mental "inboxes" and allocating a block of time for each. The

BASB method helped me refine this process by using a more recent knowledge management tool, Notion.io.

I recommend that you start with GTD and then move on to BASB. This way, you'll start quickly with a reliable and simple system that will make you a planning machine that won't forget a thing. The GTD is in sync with the brain's natural planning process, which includes:[11]

- **defining purpose and objectives;**

- **defining the outcome and deliverables of a project;**

- **brainstorming and ideation;**

- **organizing and prioritizing; and**

- **identifying the tasks and actions needed.**

This is backed by a workflow that will become second nature for processing all ideas, thoughts, tasks, promises, and more into the system. It will increase your brain's capacity and you won't have to worry so much about what you might forget. Learning this method will give you the foundation to accelerate your focus and success. I included the link to the resources website for your reference under the resources heading in this book.

Once you're comfortable with the GTD method, then you can start building your knowledge management system (KMS). This is where you store all the information you learn, making it easily retrievable for projects or tasks when needed, without relying on the depleting

---

11 David Allen, *Getting Things Done: The Art of Stress-Free Productivity*, Revised edition (New York, New York: Penguin Books, 2015).

memory capacity of our brains. BASB is one method you could use. Again, there are links to more information on the resource website, which you can access through the link provided under the resources heading of this book.

2. **Be mindful of cognitive biases**. As human beings, our brains always trick us into believing that we're always right and that we're the focal point of everything around us.[12] This can be true in how we deal with each other at work. The higher you are in the ranks, the deeper and wider an influence your behavior has throughout the organization. So, it's crucial to be mindful of and mitigate against all these biases which can influence the accuracy of your decisions. As leaders, our pride tends to get in the way of progress by rationalizing our emotional decisions and ignoring any signs of biases. This behavior often blinds us to some facts that negate our assumptions and drives us to make wrong or unfair choices. Everyone faces this challenge, but successful people learn how to be mindful of it and embrace it constructively.

For example, if you're interviewing a group of candidates, will the order in which they're scheduled influence your decision? The short answer is yes. Two psychological phenomena, primacy bias and recency bias, suggest you will lean toward the first or last candidates interviewed.

---

12 Matt Blumberg and Peter M. Birkeland, *Startup CXO: A Field Guide to Scaling up Your Company's Critical Functions and Teams* (Hoboken, New Jersey: Wiley, 2021).

Other biases to be aware of include the following:

- **Confirmation bias:** We prefer information that supports our existing beliefs. Otherwise, we dismiss it.

- **False consensus:** We believe that more people agree with us than is actually the case.

- **Status quo bias:** We believe that the current situation is optimal and we shouldn't make any changes that could cause potential losses.

- **Stereotyping bias:** We tend to oversimplify the profiling of people's qualities and values, treating them as facts.

- **Parkinson's Law of Triviality:** Our prioritization gets skewed when we see trivial issues as complex while ignoring the more pressing issues.

- **Blind spot bias:** We focus on other people's biases and ignore the fact that we have our own. In most cases, we believe we don't have biases.

- **Sunk cost fallacy:** When you decide to continue pursuing a project and invest more resources while ignoring all the facts and signs that you need to stop and mark the project as a failure.

According to David Robson's book *The Intelligence Trap*, intelligent individuals are more susceptible to biases. He also spoke about a term psychologists call "motivated reasoning," where our logic becomes influenced by our emotions, which leads us to demolish any evidence that contradicts our beliefs.[13] There are more stories and examples in the book, which I recommend you read to become better at spotting biases and avoiding their pitfalls.

---

13 David Robson, *The Intelligence Trap: Why Smart People Make Stupid Mistakes*, Paperback edition (London: Hodder & Stoughton, 2020).

Being aware of the existence of these biases and detecting them is part of the mindful stage. However, you need to build routines that raise your immunity against them—see Figure 7.

3. **Fix things right the first time**. This doesn't mean you become obsessed with perfection and avoid making mistakes. Perfectionism can be expensive and unrealistic. It can also lead to anxiety and stress. Seek to produce the *optimal outcome* with the resources available without cutting corners. It's always best to start with a prototype to test your hypotheses and then change one variable at a time.

How to Prevent Misweighting

When we give too much or too little significance to the information we have, our decisions may suffer. It's a problem with all types of bias, but these tactics can help.

	UTILITY	EXAMPLES
BLINDING	Improve judgment by eliminating the influence of stereotypes, idiosyncratic associations, and irrelevant factors.	· Orchestras have players audition behind a screen to prevent gender bias. After this became standard practice, female membership skyrocketed from 5% in 1970 to nearly 40% today. · Many professors ensure fair grading by covering up names (or asking an assistant to do so) before evaluating papers and other assignments.
CHECKLISTS	Reduce errors due to forgetfulness and other memory distortions by directing our attention to what's most relevant.	· Venture capitalists often use a set list of criteria to vet entrepreneurial pitches. · Savvy hiring managers assess candidates by conducting structured interviews (they're much more accurate predictors of performance than open-ended interviews). Because there's a standard way to rate responses, people can be easily compared on various dimensions.
ALGORITHMS	Ensure consistency by predetermining how much emphasis each piece of information will get.*	· Banks and other lenders use scoring algorithms to predict consumers' creditworthiness. · Taking a page from professional baseball, employers are starting to use algorithms in hiring. One study showed that a simple equation for evaluating applicants outperformed human judgment by at least 25%.

*Since algorithms reflect the biases of the experts who build them, it's best to combine them with other debiasing tools.

SOURCE JACK B. SOLL, KATHERINE L. MILKMAN, AND JOHN W. PAYNE
FROM "OUTSMART YOUR OWN BIASES," MAY 2015

Figure 7: How to prevent misweighting

For example, if you want to speed up the refund process in your company, you could either pressure finance to accelerate the approval process case by case, which might give you temporary results, or create a policy that empowers the frontliners to make the decision if the case meets certain guidelines. Initially, it could be a pilot phase under observation until you and the responsible stakeholders are happy with the outcome.

4. **Lead with integrity and respect; be "firm and fair."** In a position of power, it is easy to let the rush of authority go to your head and end up disrespecting colleagues, partners, or customers. However, bossing people around will not build trust. You need to communicate in a constructive manner that is respectful while remaining firm in your recommendations and views. If someone else is responsible for the outcome, you need to make sure you are being fair to them by providing nonbiased input.

   Another way of building trust is asking for and being open to constructive feedback. This will also help you become better at giving feedback, which again builds trust. Criticizing someone in public will make the person on the receiving end defensive. This will prevent them learning from the feedback you are giving. Conversely, praising publicly, as long as it is sincere, will encourage the person to do more of the same and ensure a constructive work environment which focuses on coaching and improving performance.

5. **Defer judgment on people's ideas or suggestions** to ensure that creative input is always given the consideration it deserves. What worked or failed once may not again under different circumstances. We get tempted to quickly judge a situation based on our personal experiences, rather than the conditions that caused the outcome of what worked and what did not. Confirmation bias is a major blind spot for many leaders, causing them to dismiss new ideas by assuming their failure based on limited personal experience.

6. **"Move quickly, touch lightly"**[14] to ensure you focus on what is most important now and take small steps toward continuous improvement. This approach will help you avoid being dragged down by less important tasks, which could cause the whole project to fail. This is also a best practice that Tiago Forte, the creator of Building a Second Brain, teaches to help create a system that will make sure you're always mindful of the responsibilities that may not be a high priority right now but will eventually become so. This way, you minimize the risk of forgetting a task, project, or solution that you need to prepare for some time in the future. This is the best way to navigate an environment that's fast-moving and filled with uncertainty. Learning from nature, bees and humming-birds are the most effective at this. They fly by a group of flowers, slowing down to inspect each one before touching down. They are programmed to assess the conditions, scanning for nectar and possible predators.

---

14 Tiago Forte, *Building a Second Brain: A Proven Method to Organize Your Digital Life and Unlock Your Creative Potential* (Atria Books, 2022) p. 108, Kindle Edition.

> **"Embrace a bias toward action."**[15]
>
> Tom Kelley

If the stakes are high, especially if it could lead to you or a colleague getting fired, you'll have the natural tendency to overanalyze and worry about sharing an idea or a solution or being prematurely judged for it. However, it's always best to start small with a prototype and seek feedback. That way, you don't delay working on a solution, and you'll manage people's expectations in the process, involving them in your creative process. To learn more about the creative process, I recommend you read the book *Creative Confidence* in which the founders of Ideo.com share their journey and case studies, building a team that has confidence in their creativity and transfers this culture to their customers.

> **"Life is like a game of cards. The hand that is dealt you represents determinism; the way you play it is free will."**
>
> *Attributed to Jawaharlal Nehru,*
> *India's first prime minister*

7. **Waiting for perfect conditions leads to wasted opportunities**.
   The best conditions in which to submit a proposal or start a project are when minimum required resources are available to deliver the required outcomes. There will be challenges that keep popping up as you are implementing the projects, whether they're creating a new product feature, service, or an enhancement of a process, and you'll need to deal with all of these challenges with an open mind and heart

---

15 David Kelley and Tom Kelley, *Creative Confidence: Unleashing the Creative Potential within Us All* (New York: Crown Business, 2013).

as they come. If you're worried that you'll get stuck or end up cutting corners and failing, start with a small test or a prototype to assess the viability before you proceed further and invest more time and resources. This approach is known as the Minimum Viable Philosophy. This philosophy can be applied to every type of project including products, services, processes, organizational structure, or ecosystem creation. MVP (Minimum Viable Product) is the most famous of them all in the startup world and you can find many sources to learn about it, where I have added more resources on the resources page of the book.

8. **It's about how fast your recover from a mistake**. Fear of being judged if we fail is pervasive in many cultures worldwide. However, successful founders and entrepreneurs know they are where they are because of the fast learning cycles they have had to go through by recovering from a mistake and learning from it. As Rocky Balboa says, "It's not about how hard you hit. It's about how hard you can get hit and keep moving forward.[16]

9. **Invest in your critical analytical thinking skills.** When the level of uncertainty is high and data is limited, and you have too many options to choose from, this skill will be critical to your success. The easiest approach to learn to be an effective critical thinker is to learn how deductive reasoning is used by lawyers to persuade the judge and jury to decide for or against a judgement. You can apply the same approach toward building and communicating arguments or a business case to the CEO, the CFO, partners, your board members, or customers.

---

16 *Rocky Balboa, It Ain't About How Hard You Hit*, MGM Studios, 2006, Accessed 2021, https://www.youtube.com/watch?v=kyQrl7AWeXg.

The most famous approach of effective persuasion is the Aristotelian Rhetoric, created by the Greek philosopher Aristotle. According to Aristotle, there are three components of an effective argument or communication.[17]

a) **Ethos:** using hard data and evidence to support your decision or argument.

b) **Logos:** adding credibility to your argument through case studies, historic examples of similar companies, your or colleague's track record or experience.

c) **Pathos:** tapping into the emotions of the audience or the stakeholders involved, such as customers or colleagues.

Aristotle also highlights that there are two types of proofs you can use.

a) **Inductive Reasoning:** using examples to draw conclusions. If your argument states that raising your prices will improve customer retention, then present a case study of an industry leader who succeeded in applying the same strategy and the points of similarities that will make it work for you.

b) **Deductive Reasoning:** Using observations and probability, you reverse engineer a case from high-level claim down to the premise and evidence supporting the claim. Figure 8 is a simple illustrative example of deductive reasoning.

---

17 Annette Rottenberg and Donna Haisty Winchell, *The Structure of Argument*, Eighth edition (Bedford/St. Martin's), p. 5, Kindle Edition

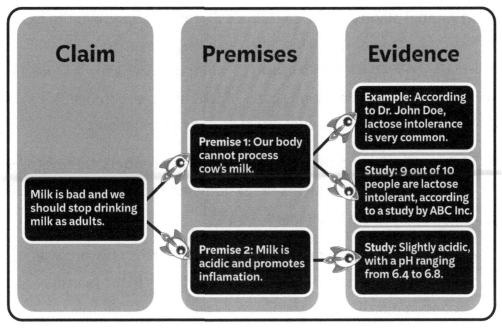

Figure 8: A simplified example of how an argument is structured

10. **Balance time spent in the weeds with time in the helicopter.** As a startup leader, it's crucial that you balance your time between diving into the details and high-level strategic thinking. Even though this sounds simple, it takes time for most leaders to find routines that help them do this.

> *"Get in the mud."*[18]
>
> Howard Schultz, former CEO of Starbucks

Also, book dedicated focus time in your calendar to review data and plans. Consider the following routines I've used for many years and work for me.

---

18 Howard Schultz, MASTERCLASS CLASS WITH HOWARD SCHULTZ Business Leadership, n.d., MasterClass.com

a) **Annual planning:** two to four blocks totaling up to eight to ten hours of focus, which includes reviewing the progress of last year, any research you have to do, strategy documents you need to write and update, hiring plans, financial projections, OKR (Objectives, Key Results) updates, and presentations.

b) **Board and senior management progress reports:** this includes project updates, incidents or risk items, and controls implemented to address such future risks.

c) **Monthly progress review:** review the progress of all projects against the annual plan and any adjustments to the plan in coordination with other colleagues and external partners.

d) **Weekly planning:** review weekly calendar, making deadlines and blocking meetings and focus times.

11. **Small improvements lead to operational excellence**. Positive, lasting innovations are achieved one step at a time through smaller projects. These can be achieved through agile project development, for example, using sprints that are two weeks in length. There are usually one or two possible solutions to the problem you are facing. Your success in achieving operational excellence depends a lot on the consistency of implementing continuous improvements toward those solutions. You should always look for ways to optimize and refine your processes, even when things are going well, because there's always something to improve, and eventually, this will help you create the ingredients of a competitive advantage that differentiates you. For example, Apple came out with music players and smartphones late in the market. Sony was already a major name

in MP3 players, and Blackberry was already dominating the smart phone market. However, due to Apple's desire for excellence in service delivery, product, and customer experience, they have been able to keep improving on their products and services month after month and year after year, differentiating themselves from their competitors to become the brand we know today.

Look for customer feedback if you're stuck and unsure what to focus on. Go through the complaints report and escalated customer support tickets. You can also interview a sample group of your customers. I'm sure you'll find ways that you can enhance a service delivered directly to your customers. If your function is not dealing directly with the product or service delivery, then you can look for enhancement opportunities that will improve the speed and quality of the output of the team members or directly contribute to the product or service delivery. For example, if you implement software for the sales staff to be able to claim business expenses such as client lunches, then you'll free the sales people from the admin work to focus on their job and bring more customers and minimize mistakes in expense claims.

Finally, it's important to remember that operational excellence is not a one-time thing, but an ongoing process that requires commitment and dedication to following processes that promote continuous improvement.

12. **Befriend your imposter syndrome.** Imposter syndrome is common in highly intelligent and self-aware individuals. Motivation coaches and authors teach us to be aware of and fight against this

force within us that brings us down through self-doubt. However, I believe it is better to embrace it as a force that will help you stress-test and refine your proposals and arguments. Embrace the uncertainty imposter syndrome brings and allow yourself to be wrong. It will make you humble, which will serve as a counter-balance to your passion. While most of your peers will consider this approach mature and collected, some will look on it as a sign of weakness. Your calmness and collectedness will prove them wrong, so do not rise to the bait.

13. **Prepare yourself for the next stage**. Many of us make the mistake of waiting for the right opportunity to come, assuming we'll have enough time to be ready. However, in reality, you need to be prepared way ahead of time to have the skills and understanding necessary to grab it. This includes building your team's capabilities for the future, not just what you need for today and the next twelve months.[19] When a need or an opportunity comes, the more prepared you are, the higher your chances of success.

To better assess whether candidates are the right fit for your team, it helps to have an operational blueprint that outlines the service delivery procedures and the role of each function in delivering the service or product to the customer. This will enable you to clearly see who fits where and what skills and capabilities you require for each role. This includes the roles and responsibilities, the special-izations you require, and your decentralization trigger points. Ideally, as you grow the number of customers in a specific market, you'll achieve a critical mass that requires you to have a dedicated local team to serve the local market. In the best case scenario,

---

19 Blumberg and Birkeland, Startup CXO. Wiley. Kindle Edition.

the team who have been working with you in the centralized pool of resources will be the future leaders, the seed, you've been grooming to build and manage the local operation in that specific country or city. To better understand what each function entails in a startup or a scale-up, I recommend reading the book *Startup CXO* by Matt Blumberg. You can find more information on this book at the resources website.

14. **Share credit for successes and take responsibility for failures.** It is essential to be fair and for your stakeholders to see you as a leader who is nurturing and collected. It is important that you spend time coaching your direct reports to become leaders who can create leaders.

You need to bring people into the spotlight when things go well and encourage them to continue the great work and inspire others. When things go wrong, take responsibility and avoid making people scapegoats for your failures (or even their failures). Giving in to your self-serving bias will spread a culture of fear which stifles innovation. Also, people will not want to work with you if you avoid taking responsibility or point fingers at others. Eventually, you will lose the support of your colleagues. If you fall into the common trap of wanting to protect your image, you will start rationalizing and justifying a punishment instead of focusing on lessons learned.

Dimension Two:
Customer Centricity

The objective in this dimension is to remain focused on the customer experience when delivering value directly and indirectly. This applies to everyone, whether they are responsible for customer experience, product development, finance, human resources, legal, or general administration.

15. **Ensure you always manage customer expectations**. Explain to the customer what you can deliver and delve deeper into their goal or the problem they are trying to solve. In other words, build empathy within the team so they can build services that are highly valued by the customers. For example, in one of the projects I worked on, we introduced a way for customers to get in touch via WhatsApp rather than the phone, which they preferred, and also saved money by ditching an unnecessary expense for the business. I was bold in removing the phone numbers and introducing WhatsApp instead because we did it incrementally after speaking to a sample

selection of our customers and found out that they don't like waiting on the phone, and prefer to have the answers on WhatsApp so they can refer to them later.

16. **Get to the root of customer personas**. Profiling customers using their habits, goals, resources, beliefs, priorities, and other levers will help you build a better understanding of who you are serving and what they need. For example, do they want a quick solution or a human being on the end of the line? What's more important to them? This will help you make decisions based on data rather than assumptions.

17. **Establish internal service level agreements (SLAs)** to ensure that frontline employees have the support they need to resolve customer issues on time and effectively. You're not going to get it right 100% of the time, but a 95–99% success rate is an excellent target. To ensure that internal support teams share the same level of accountability as frontline teams, it is essential to create internal SLAs and a measurement system used by all departments. It will make work more transparent and help function heads align their OKRs and KPIs toward the needs of customers.

18. **Set customer expectations**. Only ever promise what you can deliver, and strive to exceed expectations. It is easy to offer phone support or costly features because that's what others are doing. When your product or service is unique, customers will come to you because you are different and you fit their needs, not because you are perfect and offer everything.

19. **Prevent recurring issues**. Analyze all customer complaints to identify their frequent problems and implement enhancements that will prevent them from happening, if possible. Otherwise, put features that make the fix fast. For example, if most of your customers forget to pay their monthly fees on time and get their accounts blocked because of nonpayment, then a solution would be to automate the payment collection by storing their cards on your system.

20. **Focus on the right customers**. You must accept that you cannot please everyone. Narrowing your focus to target the right customers will be a better investment of your time and effort and yield a higher return because these customers value and appreciate that you are trying to solve their problems. Those whom your company cannot satisfy can leave quickly and easily, allowing you to concentrate on the right customers.

21. **Seek customer feedback**, whether through random email samples, chat history reviews, or listening to customer support calls. Track it, especially escalated cases, and review it regularly as a group. Leaders from internal support functions, such as engineering or finance, should join customer feedback meetings to understand the challenges the company is facing and to assist by proposing fixes and implementing solutions.

22. **Empower your employees to solve problems on their own**. In low-risk cases, have a policy that gives your employees the freedom to make decisions themselves without getting approval from their line manager. For example, if customers tried the product within the first thirty days, and they're eligible for a refund if they're not happy

with the product, then empower the customer support representatives to immediately approve the refund for the customer without having to send a request to the finance department and wait for approval. This will reduce the delays in service delivery and will free the finance team to work on their core function.

This approach frees you and other leaders up from being a bottleneck in the service delivery process, and through these controls and policies, you end up improving the service delivery.

Mistakes will happen but it won't matter in the bigger scheme of things. For example, banks issue credit cards to customers who are eligible even though they know that around 1–5% of their card holders will fail at paying back their amounts due. Despite that, they keep making it easy to give more credit cards to more customers, because despite these losses, the profit margins they make absorb all the losses. So they do assess the credit card defaults as an acceptable loss.

Do your best to keep controls in place to prevent deviation from the process and monitor the results periodically to ensure you control the risk and spot opportunities for improvement.

"To build an agile operation that fosters a culture of operational excellence and innovation, it's critical to move away from being boss-centric culture to build a customer-centric culture."

Professor Stefanos Zenios, Stanford GSB

Dimension Three:

Culture and Team

Creating a high-performing and high-integrity culture within companies is an ongoing challenge. You must be vigilant and constantly aware of the culture you are fostering as you build and grow the company. It is a grinding and complex task but also very rewarding to the organization in the long run. Some of the actions that will help you build a self-sustaining, strong culture include leading by example, recognizing proactivity, and rewarding positive results. Creating the right culture will give your company a solid foundation.

23. **Promote constructive feedback**. As a leader, it's essential to ensure that the employees respect each other's feedback and opinions. A useful approach you could take is to encourage them to start their sentences with "I like" or "I wish."[20]

---

20 Kelley and Kelley, *Creative Confidence*.

Implementing a practice of one person speaking at a time without interruptions is the first step in fostering a respectful culture. This will encourage the quiet employees to speak during meetings, creating a more inclusive environment.

Praise people who come up with ideas and give constructive feedback. Avoid public criticism and make sure no one shoots anyone's ideas down without a rational reason. As a leader, it's your responsibility to create a safe environment by communicating that there are no bad ideas. You can break the ice by asking for the craziest ideas first and volunteering to be the first to go through a crazy, unrealistic idea. This will teach people to respect suggestions they disagree with and allow them to practice delivering a counterargument or justification.

24. **Keep meetings agenda-specific and focused**. Meetings that have a loose agenda and no discussion points to go through tend to be unproductive and end up wasting everyone's time. Employees will start to resent these meetings, and some employees will avoid calling for meetings even if they were really important, due to the stigma they have.

Some best practices I use include the following:

- End meetings very quickly, as soon as the agenda points are done.
- List the agenda within the calendar invites.
- Make the meetings short on the calendar invite.
- Start on time (especially for the routine small meetings). When the meeting is a large group involving external stakeholders, it's acceptable in most cultures to wait for around five minutes until everyone shows up.

•If the time isn't enough for the subject raised and it requires multiple stakeholders to be involved, schedule another meeting as a working session specifically for that subject.

When coached in the right manner, this pragmatic approach will become instilled within the team. It also will start spreading into other teams beyond the function you're responsible for.

> *"Each CXO believes that their part of the business is the most important part. And they make a compelling set of arguments."*
>
> Matt Blumberg, Three times CEO, and Author of *Startup CEO* and *Startup CXO*

25. **Put the needs of the business before the needs of a department**. As a leader, it is critical to your success that you always think as a partner and not as an employee. You must always prioritize company objectives and the needs of the business, which requires collaboration with your peers. For example, you want a budget allocated to your team so you can automate some accounting procedures, while your colleague is asking for the same budget to launch into a new market, which could eventually yield the funds to pay for your request within six months. In that case, you should step back and propose that their project is prioritized.

26. **Diversify teams based on personalities and skills**. Use one of the many personality tests widely available online to better understand what drives your employees. This could result in increased productivity, innovation, and better decisions being

made. I have been using a simple approach since 2017 called the "Pioneer, Driver, Integrator, and Guardian"[21] framework, which defines four personality types as follows:

a) **Pioneers**: These leaders want to implement innovative ideas, don't like overthinking or overanalyzing or being delayed. They focus on the big picture and tend to be okay with taking risks.

b) **Integrators**: They are focused on bringing teams together and gaining consensus. They contribute significantly to building a sense of belonging in the company. They usually get irritated by cynical people.

c) **Drivers**: They are result-oriented and data-driven. They keep discussions focused on results and derived decisions.

d) **Guardians**: They want stability and hesitate to take risks. They need data and time to analyze it before making a recommendation or a decision. They are uncomfortable rushing through important and risky decisions.

This approach has been created based on scientific studies. The creators of this framework, Dr. Suzanne Vickberg, a social-personality psychologist, and Kim Christfort, a business coach, consulted with biological anthropologist Helen Fisher of Rutgers University, who specializes in researching brain chemistry in romantic relationships.

---

21 Kim Christfort Suzanne M. Johnson Vickberg, "Pioneers, Driver, Integrators, and Guardians," *Harvard Business Review*, April 2017.

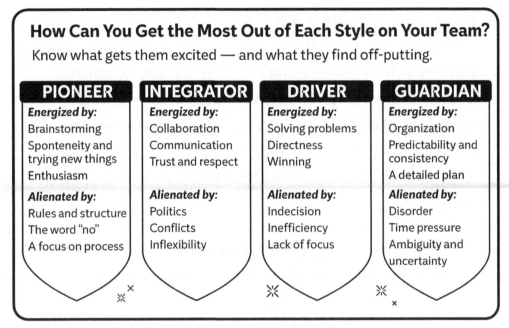

How Can You Get the Most Out of Each Style on Your Team?
Know what gets them excited — and what they find off-putting.

PIONEER	INTEGRATOR	DRIVER	GUARDIAN
Energized by:	*Energized by:*	*Energized by:*	*Energized by:*
Brainstorming	Collaboration	Solving problems	Organization
Sponteneity and trying new things	Communication	Directness	Predictability and consistency
Enthusiasm	Trust and respect	Winning	A detailed plan
Alienated by:	*Alienated by:*	*Alienated by:*	*Alienated by:*
Rules and structure	Politics	Indecision	Disorder
The word "no"	Conflicts	Inefficiency	Time pressure
A focus on process	Inflexibility	Lack of focus	Ambiguity and uncertainty

Figure 9: Preferences of each personality

They have also collaborated with molecular biologist Lee Silver of Princeton to apply statistical models to group people based on patterns. Around 190,000 people have completed the assessment, more than 3,000 lab tests have been conducted with leaders and teams, and interactive sessions spanning ninety minutes to three days have been held. The outcome was increased productivity and innovation, and improved decision-making.

There are other personality tests that you can explore, including Myer-Briggs Type Indicator, Five Factor Model, and Strengths Finder.

To learn more about applying this practically, check the resources website mentioned at the beginning of this book.

27. **Ensure introverts are heard**. Many introverts are intelligent and have great ideas which they might not express without encouragement or the right environment. They can also be coached to become great project and team leaders. Most introverts are observant and collected, very useful qualities for solving problems. They effectively drive change by empowering their team members to become more proactive and involved, which enhances the probability of success.

There's a general assumption that extroverts make better leaders. However, in an experiment conducted by three professors in the US, where two different groups of students were tasked to produce and sell T-shirts, the teams with introverted leaders sold 28% more T-shirts than the teams with extroverted leaders. They discovered that extroverted leaders stifle proactivity because they feel threatened by it.[22]

- The following are some suggested actions to encourage introverts to speak up and be more involved:

- When having standup meetings, ask the team to take turns in leading the meeting agenda.

- In meetings, make sure the meeting leader of the day asks every person if they have anything they want to speak about.

- Coach introverts on speaking in meetings encouraging them to organize their thoughts through speaking points and proposals.

---

22 Adam M Grant, Francesca Gino, and David A Hofmann, "The Hidden Advantages of Quiet Bosses," n.d. *Harvard Business Review*, December 2010.

28. **Ensure governance policies are implemented and followed**. This will empower CXOs, managers, and other leaders in the organization to make decisions while at the same time holding them accountable and ensuring KPIs are fairly evaluated.

29. **Adopt and implement a RACI mindset**. It is critical that leaders have the ability to make sound decisions and encourage their team to work together instead of working in silos. RACI is a framework that helps create a shared understanding of who is responsible for which tasks in a project, similar to a departmental decision matrix. RACI stands for:

   a) **Responsible:** The person responsible for getting the task done. This person works on the task.

   b) **Accountable:** This person is responsible for the entire job being completed.

   c) **Consulted:** These are individuals, subject matter experts, or stakeholders, such as function owners, whom you or the project manager need to consult for their sign-off.

   d) **Informed:** These individuals must stay informed of any process changes or updates. They could be function heads or managers who take responsibility for an action or keeping the customers informed of any changes.

   A RACI is usually a table or matrix that includes people's names and functions. For more information on how a RACI matrix is used, visit the resources website of the book.

30. **Hire "A" Players for your critical positions**. As you are scaling up the operations of a company, it is vital to hire leaders who have experience doing so, who are subject matter experts, who are passionate, and who know how to design value streams. You must hire leaders you can rely on who won't become the weak link within your organizational structure.

31. **Hire and keep the right people on your team**. Maintaining a positive culture within your ranks is critical to the success of scaling up, decentralizing, and localizing your company's functions. You have to hire, train, and retain emerging leaders who can think as designers and coaches for their teams.

   When a person is not showing the potential to learn and grow with the upcoming needs of the business, you have to replace them. You have to be open with them and accept that when you hire people who are not up to the standard, they will hold everyone back. You need to bring in someone more qualified to take the company to the next level.

32. **Neutralize any "sense of entitlement."** Most employees who join a startup early do so because they see the potential to accelerate their career. Often, they have a sense of entitlement that they should grow as leaders instead of being assigned to work under new managers. It's best to get ahead of any dissatisfaction by explaining to them how they can grow as the company grows. During coaching sessions, you can help them prepare for when their opportunity to become a leader arises.

33. Detect and diffuse the root cause of power withdrawal symptoms. As you scale up the company, you have to bring more specialists on board and split specific roles. This will be met by resistance from employees who feel these changes threaten their existing roles. When you ask them to train a new peer to take ownership of areas they used to own, they will suffer from power withdrawal syndrome.

Stanford professor Jeffrey Pfeffer, author of the book *Power*, explains that the symptoms are similar to those of drug withdrawal and could lead to deep depression[23]. Therefore, the best solution is to support the transition by helping those employees focus on the big picture and continue developing as a specialist in their field. It would be best to mix coaching and micromanagement until the roles are clear.

In an ideal scenario, both employees will find their state of flow and remain motivated and eager to grow. However, you have to address the power withdrawal symptoms that the old employee may have as if you are taking them off a drug. You can always prepare for such a situation by making sure that you have a centralized file-sharing system so that one person doesn't have ownership of particular documents or knowledge.

34. Be graceful and fair when firing an employee. If someone within your ranks needs to be more productive and has proven they can't be coached, you must let them go. This is especially true if this person brings toxic behavior into the workplace that affects the motivation of others. If they are skilled and have a great

---

23 Jeffrey Pfeffer, *Power: Why Some People Have It and Others Don't* (New York, NY: HarperBusiness, 2010).

work ethic, but you believe they could do better in another role in another function, you should facilitate that move so they can still add value to the organization. It will foster a positive culture if handled respectfully and with integrity, and show employees that you care about their growth.

35. **Make daily standup meetings mandatory**. This is especially important if the team is working remotely or in a hybrid setup. For these meetings to work, parameters must be set in place so they are short and effective. Ideally, meetings should be held in the mornings, include eight to eleven team members, and last between five and fifteen minutes with a hard stop so your team can continue to be effective. If more time is needed, you can schedule another meeting, including only the people who need to be there.

    Keep meetings more frequent but short, and follow the agenda. The agenda must be limited and focused on core questions to update you on critical issues and ensure your priorities are current. Some suggested questions include: *What did you do yesterday? What will you do today? Are there any blockers?* This ensures that people are synchronized and connected and that everyone, including introverts, can be heard. Let the team take turns leading standup meetings.

36. **Implement a responsibilities matrix**. Having a responsibility matrix for routine work is essential. It defines the roles of those who own each area of the internal knowledge base and keep it up to date. It will give people a sense of ownership in the areas they are responsible for. Also, assigning secondary and tertiary owners is a good practice to ensure business continuity.

Activity	Primary	Secondary	Tritiary
Activity A	Person A	Person B	Person C
Activity B	Person A	Person A	Person B
Activity C	Person B	Person C	Person A

Figure 10: A responsibility matrix template

A responsibility matrix, also called an authority matrix, is a policy document that outlines who is responsible for what tasks and whose approval is needed for that work. It can be as simple as a table, as shown in the figure on the next page.

It is common to step on toes when taking on new initiatives and miss some critical functions in the decision-making process. Sometimes you have to move fast, which requires approvals immediately. Logically, the risk involved should determine how long these decisions take.

Most approvals are sanity checks rather than actual assessments. For example, consider the process of changing the price of a product, which requires proper planning and involvement from other departments. This cannot be assessed at the same speed as the need to send a mailer out to all customers because you have a product defect or your systems are down, which requires fast, effective responses.

When you involve someone unnecessarily, just out of courtesy, it wastes their time. They will likely not see it as being courteous. To maximize the number of fast and accurate responses and decisions, build your own authority matrix that becomes a living document.

37. **Conduct skip-level meetings routinely**. As the company grows, it will become more challenging for you to meet everyone. Skip-level meetings are those with your direct report's direct reports. They are a great way to get to know younger employees and to keep an eye on the big picture. All leaders and managers should conduct skip-level meetings, and it is crucial that you coach them on conducting these correctly. Be open about why these meetings are essential for the company's greater good. As we all build natural biases as human beings, we become desensitized to our line managers. Skipping a level breaks our routines and allows us to receive and share fresh feedback. Common agenda items could include asking what things the junior employee would like leadership to stop doing, start doing, and continue doing.

38. **Implement periodic 360-degree feedback performance evaluations**. This means all company employees will have the opportunity to receive feedback from peers, reporting employees, line managers, customers, and vendors if applicable. They'll also have the opportunity to give feedback about their peers. This will help uncover opportunities for improvement within the team and reveal specific areas of strength. It's a good way to remain proactive toward uncovering any emerging trends that impact the culture beneath the surface of your everyday visible interactions.

39. **Clarify what makes a mistake acceptable**. When you communicate that mistakes are part of innovation, you have to be clear what you mean by this. It's not acceptable to fail due to negligence, but taking a calculated risk which doesn't come off is a learning experience, and it is about how fast you recover from the mistake.

40. Engaged employees are committed employees. When you match people to what they like doing and give them a safe space to make their mark, they will likely commit to the role. As you scale up your operation, you will need passionate and dedicated individuals and leaders. Investing time in coaching and ensuring people fit their roles will pay off in the long run. In other words, you need to align people's values and passions with the objectives of the business.

> *"People don't like to be told what to do ... when we are told to do something, our natural reaction is to push back."*
>
> Jocko Willink, former Navy Seal

Willink says that on most of the military missions he led, he never had to tell people what to do in detail because everyone knew what was expected out of them and how they could add value and work together to complete their mission and survive[24]. His secret to success was him giving clarity about their roles and the freedom to make decisions per the decision-making framework that the team trusted and agreed on. The same goes for a scalable business. When your leaders are committed to and understand their roles in building a successful and scalable company, giving them the freedom to make their own decisions within a clear framework creates a strong team that delivers results against the uncertainties of startups.

---

24 Jocko Willink, MASTERCLASS CLASS WITH JOCKO WILLINK Critical Leadership Training, n.d., MasterClass.com.

41. **Building trust among team members prevents conflict and promotes collaboration**. When you assign teams to a project, holding the leader accountable for the outcome and the team accountable for supporting them, everyone comes together more effectively. They know that when their turn comes to lead, they will need the same support that they are giving the current leader.

42. **Be more inclusive, less intrusive**. When trying to implement new changes and win the necessary support, it is essential to give stakeholders a sense of ownership. You can do that by allowing them to help find an overall solution, especially if the bottleneck is in their department or function. Being forceful and dictating what they must do will create resistance to any idea and spread a dysfunctional culture that lacks trust. They'll most likely perceive you as someone who doesn't respect their capabilities and is gunning to replace them. You have to be mindful to the fact that people want to work with people they like. From experience, taking a coaching approach of leading them toward the answer through questions and constructive feedback is the best approach that works most of the time.

43. **Encourage support functions to be partners (not just guardians)**. Most support functions follow a process with controls that protect the business. As your company grows, so does the importance of these controls. Function heads tend to operate as guardians rather than solutions seekers. It is essential to collaborate with these leaders and guide them on how they can safely contribute to the company's innovation.

One basic example is in finance, the support department with the most to protect. You can collaborate with the controller to set limits under which their approval is not needed. This will speed the refund process for customers, empower frontline employees to make decisions, and gives the financial controller room to learn about the impact of policymaking so they can take better-calculated risks.

44. **Turn your values into a mantra**. During daily standup meetings, have people recite the team's values. This will ensure that everyone is familiar with them and is prepared to repeat and explain them. It will also encourage people to refer to the values when the situation calls for it, and it involves team members who are usually quiet. It also will help the loud ones become more inclusive and empathetic toward their colleagues.

Some define a mantra as a phrase that is repeated silently before entering a challenging context.[25] However, my definition differs. Instead of making it a silent and personal practice, treat the team as a single organism. The mantra is specific to the team's mission and function. Each department might have minor modifications. This becomes more powerful when the team members are all working remotely or in hybrid settings.

For example, one team I had responsibility for I asked the person leading the daily standup meeting agenda to recite our values in less than thirty seconds. This empowered team members to engage,

---

25 Deborah Gruenfeld, Melissa Jones Briggs, and Lori Nishiura Mackenzie, "Using a Mantra to Be a More Inclusive Leader," *Harvard Business Review*, 2022.

offering suggestions and taking initiatives. Yes, it was awkward at the beginning, and people resisted. However, three years on and the practice is still taking place without my involvement.

45. **Maintain a success log**. A success log is a project list revised by function heads who meet periodically to review project statuses, new project requests, and prioritization. This will protect your company from falling into the trap of distrust or rivalry among departments. It focuses planning discussions on what value has been created for the customer and how it contributes to the company's objectives, whether that's process automation, taking on board some new data, or adding a new feature to fix a problem. All can give you the edge over your competitors. This pipeline of improvements will be your company's North Star.

If there is already distrust, you need to have a candid discussion with function leaders and air all your concerns constructively and respectfully to find some common ground and work toward the greater good of the company.

To build your list of projects, focus on the customer's pain points. What are they complaining about? Look at customer interview transcripts and competitive market reports. Then, evaluate each pain point against agreed upon criteria, such as availability of resources and potential revenue growth. Business tools such as the RICE framework can help with this.

Reviewing the completed projects or initiatives will ensure trust grows among departments or functions.

46. Make sure concerns are aired in the right environment.

To make sure that concerns are aired respectfully and handled positively, ensure you are in the right setting to discuss concerns. This will diffuse miscommunication and enable you to build trust among functions and departments.

To succeed at setting the right conditions to ensure your concern is received constructively, you need to consider the following questions:

- Is this concern rational, for the collective good of the business, and not diluted with personal feelings and biases?

- Is it better to conduct it in private, one-to-one, or in a group meeting? Would someone feel insulted if employees reporting to them were in the meeting when concern is aired? Would they feel offended if their line manager was in the meeting and could see it as an unnecessary escalation?

- What wording, if used, will communicate the concern accurately without causing a colleague to perceive it as an attack on them?

- Is it better to do it in writing to take the emotions out of it?

- Is there a way to frame it as a collective issue you all need to solve?

There are more questions you'll come up with as you continue dealing with the challenges of addressing operational concerns with your colleagues. This principle also applies to any supplier or partner relationship.

47. Invest in formal and informal training. Formal training, such as in-person or online training programs, certification programs, or academic training programs, is essential to enable employees to progress in their careers, stay fresh with their knowledge, and continue contributing more to the company.

Informal training, such as coaching sessions, brown bag lunches, on-job-training, or reading a book, is important too. The unstructured nature of informal training activities gives the employees the flexibility to learn quickly what's needed to get the job done without having to carve out hours. It also allows the employees to share knowledge and tap into the collective knowledge of the organization.

	Pros	Cons
Formal Training	Higher absorption rate due to the high focus and engagement.	Requires planning ahead of time, because as a startup you have a limited number of employees and cash, having a dedicated time out of the office requires planning and coordination with colleagues.
Informal Training	Can be done more frequently and in small dedicated time slots	Requires discipline to add dedicated times in the calendar and stick to them. For example, if you don't book a time to read a book, you'll always get busy and keep pushing this timeslot for later.

Figure 11: Pros and Cons of Formal and Informal Training

To get the most out of all training sessions, leaders must coach their teams to apply what they learned on the job so they can grow and become more valuable team members. Informal training activities are important, as many startups lack the time and cash for formal training activities. This is especially true if the company is going through bridge funding stages and trying to extend its cash runway until the next round of funding.

Purchasing courses on Udemy is one option that works well. However, you need to have group accountability, where employees have a target date to complete the course.

You could also try holding brown-bag meetings, where employees bring their lunches along for some instruction by a subject matter expert or one of the leaders. This can also work for remote staff if you get everyone to turn on their cameras and be present in video.

As you can see in the chart below (Figure 12), training your team members will help them contribute more value in designing and scaling the company. They can also grow to take on more responsibilities as leaders.

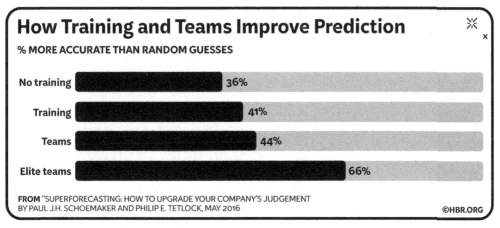

Figure 12: Training improves accuracy in decision-making

48. Ensure team member diversity. Diverse teams of people with different experiences, genders, and ethnicities will always have a more lasting impact. Many studies have proven that diverse teams deliver better performance, innovative enhancements, and attract more talent due to the inclusive culture.

49. Hold business leaders accountable for deliverables and integrity metrics. There is a saying, "Freedom without control leads to abuse." You need an environment where people are held to account for their actions. So, when you implement OKRs and empower leaders to take control of their deliverables (key results), they have fewer excuses for not achieving their goals. Including integrity metrics ensures that team members are not pressured to cut corners or stray from the right path, especially if they are in emerging markets where bribery is rife.

Dimension Four: Process Improvement and Optimization

When it comes to maintaining operational harmony among team members, processes, and technologies, it's crucial that everyone is on the same page. Each member must know their part and be able to communicate effectively with the rest of the team. This ensures everything runs smoothly and efficiently, leading to better outcomes. Whether you're working on a small project or a large-scale operation, it's vital to prioritize harmony and communication to ensure that everyone is working toward the same goal.

50. Follow the minimum viable optimization (MVO) system. I developed the MVO framework to help you strip out any unnecessary steps toward achieving the minimum acceptable and viable outcome for your situation. You have to keep in mind that the aim is not to find the perfect path, because that doesn't exist. Some might argue that it does, but we don't need a "perfect" solution because it's overkill and wastes valuable time.

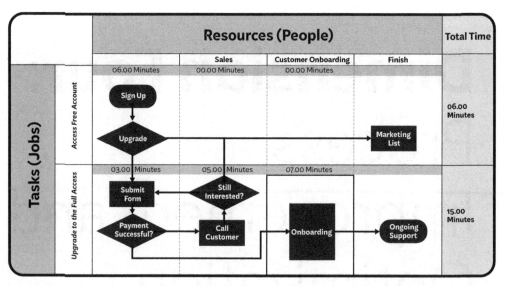

Figure 13: Example of process mapping

The MVO framework is inspired by the minimum viable product (MVP) philosophy. It is an extension of the design thinking framework (which I explain later in principle 53) as it adopts the same useful mindset of speaking to users and customers and testing hypotheses. The MVO framework will delve deeper into optimizing process design by maximizing the time, resources, and capacity at your disposal.

For example, let's say your conversion rate from website signup to paying customer is 5%, but you believe it should be 20% based on benchmarking with competitors and similar services. However, jumping by 15% in one month seems unrealistic. So, you start looking at the points of friction in the conversion process. Is it the form-filling process, the requirements, or the type of customer you're attracting? In this situation, using the MVO framework, you'll take the following activities:

a. **Build a strategic framework document**: State the goal, the objectives, the deliverables, and the timeline. Make sure the deliverables are realistic. An example of a deliverable would be "increase the conversion rate from 5% to 10%" instead of 15%, which could be too high. Also, the timeline of the pilot shouldn't exceed two weeks from the date of launch.

b. **Assess the options and prioritize** them based on impact, resource consumption, and risk of failure. You can score them if you like. The aim is to give you a better understanding of the return you'll see from your efforts. Keep testing and assessing the outcome.

c. **Maintain clear visibility of the outcome:** Avoid changing too many variables in a process flow at the same time because that will dilute the outcome and it will take you longer to understand what influenced the outcome. If Spotify wanted to increase the monthly conversion rate from free to paid premium customers, changing the color of the checkout page, adding exclusive songs to paid customers, and running a marketing campaign will all help increase the conversion rate. However, you won't know which one really gave you the highest impact because you implemented all of them at the same time, and you won't know which one you should double down on.

Mapping your processes and calculating your capacity in this way will give you a better feeling of what approach will yield better results. I built my own version as part of the MVO toolkit. You can watch the tutorial and download the template in the resources website of the book.

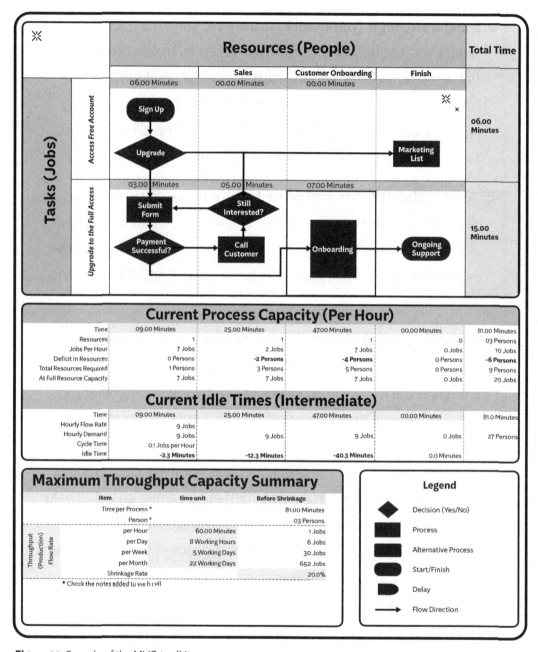

Figure 14: Sample of the MVO toolkit

51. **Change one variable at a time**. When testing a possible solution, it's best to only change one variable at a time to ensure you don't dilute the outcome and minimize the noise. I use the analogy of noise, because when you have many musical instruments playing the same piece of music but are not coordinated, it just becomes noise that you can enjoy or understand as a song, but once each instrument's output has been analyzed and timed correctly in the full song, the song will turn into an enjoyable piece of art. The same applies to designing processes and delivering value to the customers.

When under pressure, it's easy to cut corners if you're in a hurry. However, cutting corners could become more expensive and cause more delays in the long run. For example, you're producing a popular peanut butter brand with specific ingredients and you decide to substitute one of the ingredients because your usual supplier doesn't provide it anymore. So instead of going and looking for the exact same ingredient brand or using an alternative you have tested before to deliver the exact same taste, you use an untested generic brand and deliver it to the customers. This could hurt your brand if your customers realize your peanut butter doesn't taste the same or if new customers who purchased it because of a recommendation talk badly about the taste.

I have often heard, "We tried it, and it didn't work." Then, I find out they were changing more than one variable at a time. For example, if you want to reduce one step in a process, there are many variables you have to account for, such as: *Who's the person you'll be training to complete the steps? Are you eliminating the step itself? What are the ramifications of removing such a step? Did you assess the risks and involve the stakeholders if the risks were high? How can you turn a gamble into a calculated guess?*

If you still struggle with understanding the concept of this principle, I suggest learning more about how A/B testing works as a research method. A/B testing is an easy concept to understand that could work for you. Let's imagine, you are onboarding customers through a form with seven steps, and 50% of the applicants stop at step three of the form. You look at the form, and you realize that you're asking them to share a description of their line of business. So your objective is to enable the maximum number of applicants to complete step three. To achieve that objective, you have the following options:

a) Remove step three from the form.

b) Create a drop-down for the applicants to choose from.

c) Let them input the website address, build a crawler that collects information from their website, and then, through artificial intelligence, fill in step three for them.

d) Move step three to step seven in the queue.

So, to know which option would deliver the highest completion rate, you need to follow a structured approach in testing them. If you implement option B and D together, then you won't know which one really worked and whether it would've worked better if you made one change at a time. So you take a group of customers with similar profiles, you first launch option A and option B, you test them, then you select the one that has delivered a better result. If option B worked, then you compare options B and C. If B has a better conversion, then you compare B against option D and choose the best one between the two. Creating focus groups of customers and interviewing them might introduce other options

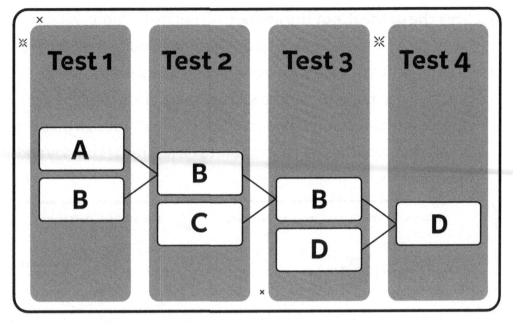

Figure 15: Example of a Simplified A/B Testing Flow

in the process. My advice, apply the concept at the beginning without getting into the details of A/B Testing.

52. **Ensure your data is sound and accessible**. The quality and frequency of the data you receive are critical to ensure you make more accurate and timely decisions. This will help you prioritize the right objectives and know what is happening and what needs to be done to achieve your goals.

    For example, having accurate and timely data on customer churn is important because it will provide insight into the reasons customers are leaving and when. You could ask them to fill out a closure request form or go through an exit interview. In a previous position, I was repeatedly receiving churn data that was two to three months old. I realized that it didn't have accurate timestamps but was based on the last update received. I couldn't act effectively on this information.

53. Seek the optimal, not the perfect. An optimal solution will have some imperfections that can be forgiven but will still hit the main objectives. I have seen many leaders spending too much time trying to perfect every aspect of their project, resulting in a delayed and overcomplicated product. That's why design thinking or kaizen approaches teach you how to deliver results quickly and incrementally.

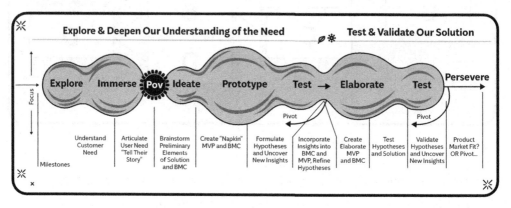

Figure 16: Innovation process taught by Stanford GSB

For example, design thinking is a lean, scientific approach to developing data-backed solutions that work. In the figure below, you can see the process flow of developing a hypothesis, then prototyping a solution. After a few cycles of testing and improving, a viable solution is reached which is proven to work.[26]

Let's say you want to reduce the customer churn for a subscription-based project management software. You conduct interviews with customers who are cancelling your service and discover that they are leaving for three main reasons:

---

26 Stefanos Zenios, "DESIGN THINKING AND LEAN STARTUP: A PROCESS TO DESIGN, TEST, AND LAUNCH YOUR STARTUP," n.d.

- Better price offered by a competitor (20%);

- Missing integration with QuickBooks (40%);

- Report generation is difficult (40%).

Which root cause will you focus on? How will you prioritize them? Which one is the fastest and easiest to solve? Let's assume you want to solve the first problem.

- **Perfect:** Introduce flexible packages where the customer can mix their own bundle of features.

- **Optimal:** Offer a discount if you subscribe for two years instead of one.

The first solution is a great long-term project. It would take time to build a model, obtain approval, and commission the engineering team to complete it. The optimal option will yield immediate results. It offers a quick remedy while you work incrementally on the ideal option. Even that can be broken down into milestones to test what packages would be attractive to customers.

54. **Make work visible**. This allows everyone on the team to see what tasks are in the queue, the team's progress, and where there may be potential roadblocks or bottlenecks. This improves communication, collaboration, and accountability within the team. Work can be made visible through a project management tool like Trello or Asana, creating a shared spreadsheet or document that outlines tasks and progress. Or you could use a whiteboard with sticky notes representing tasks. Choose a method that everyone is comfortable using.

It's important to keep things up to date to ensure that everyone has the most accurate information and can make informed decisions. It also promotes a trusting culture, encouraging creativity and innovation in a company, and minimizes room for silos to form.

55. **There are always multiple solutions, never only one**. There are always good options to choose from, but only some will be optimal. Keep an open mind to your team's and peers' suggestions. Tap into the collective intelligence of your team. If you don't have the right skillset on your team, look at the expertise in other teams. If you still have no luck, take a leap and learn as you go. Fix issues as you face them. Also, if it's a critical project, you can find a freelance expert to advise you.

56. **Eliminate silos among functions**. Silos are created when simple tasks, recurring requests, and sign-offs get stuck for approvals by one person instead of delegating the decision-making process to the rest of the team through implementing policies and controls. Silos hinder the speed of service delivery and make the team less proactive and more reactive in solving a customer problem because you're making them dependent on the decision made by someone else, and it's also communicating to them that they are not trustworthy to make decisions.

At the center of silos, you'll find someone who's thriving on the inertia that the power of being needed as the sole approver and decider. I cover this in more detail in SAUS principle number 33, **Detect and diffuse the root cause of power withdrawal symptoms**.

From a business continuity perspective, every decision and process has to be free from the dependency on one or two people only. An internal knowledge base has to be available and accessible for every function. The knowledge base includes the procedures, training materials, SLAs, internal escalation process, and all other key information required for running an uninterrupted, smooth operation.

Every process must have primary owners and two to three levels of deputies. Principle 36, **Implement a responsibilities matrix**, covers how the ownership of these areas is delegated and built. All passwords and credentials must be securely locked and accessible to all the key managers and supervisors. If a password of a tool is forgotten, any one of the authorized employees can access and reset the password, updating everyone within the team.

It is natural for many employees to want to feel important and indispensable and create alliances and clusters, especially as the company grows. In the Middle East, tribal thinking is very common among the locals and the expats who live in the region. One way to diffuse such a clustering is to make sure that there's enough diversity of nationalities, which works well for business continuity.

Silo seeders are typically those who have been at the company since the startup or seed stage. They were likely initially leading several functions or fulfilling multiple roles. As the company grew, some of their responsibilities were reassigned to specialists, which made the silo seeders feel insecure and defensive. To protect their role, they started hiding information and putting themselves at the center of every decision.

The danger of this attitude is it fosters a lack of trust and rivalry among departments. It creates single points of failure because the policies are not followed or absent. By hoarding information and keeping it to themselves, these lonely geniuses can cripple operations.

There's a proverb attributed to Lord Acton, a British historian and politician, "all power tends to corrupt, and absolute power corrupts absolutely." There's another quote that I can't recall where I heard, which really rings true "Freedom without control leads to abuse." When you have no controls in place to ensure knowledge is shared and transparent, information bullies will end up creating silos and disrespecting SLAs.

There are many ways you can break these silos, including creating and tracking SLAs among departments and offering incentives for completing tasks within the cross-functional SLAs.

To learn more about his subject, I suggest reading books on change management including *The Five Dysfunctions of a Team* by Patrick Lencioni.

57. **Use activity metrics to drive daily and weekly actions**. More than just monthly performance reviews using KPIs and OKRs are needed to coordinate a team and maximize its chances of success. Daily metrics and schedules will help you develop a team of productive individuals who work intentionally and are likely to achieve a state of flow.

Let's say agent has a quarterly target of onboarding 500 customers. You can break this down to the activities needed over those three months. *How many follow-ups does the agent need to make? Cold calls? How many applications do they need to process? How many training sessions they need to conduct?* List the answers and set daily and weekly targets for each to help them achieve their performance goals and objectives.

58. **Beware the past success bias trap**. It's also known as "Outcome Bias." Applying the same solution to a problem just because it worked before could limit innovation and, at times, lead to failure. When solving a new process, product, or strategy problem, use everything around you for inspiration to ask the right strategic questions. If an approach has worked for you or someone else in a similar situation, it's worth putting high on your priorities as a solution, but you have to be open to the fact it might not work this time. Many variables change over time, such as the available technologies, people around you, what competitors offer in the market, budget constraints, and more. That's why you need to keep an open mind to making new discoveries through proto-typing before fully deploying a new process or solution.

For example, let's assume you're working for a fintech startup and you have a new customer application you need to process through collecting all identification and verification documents. As the number of applications grows and the size of the team grows, you need to create a system that will help your team remain organized and for your supervisors to monitor the performance of the team members on a daily, weekly, and monthly basis. Based on an old experience, you were using Excel sheets to assign people lists of customers and then track them, and that worked. So you want to implement the same solution. Someone from your team suggests making the applications available visually through a Kanban Board. Will you dismiss this proposal because Excel documents worked before, or are you open to learning more about how Kanbans are implemented and giving it a shot?

59. **Be intentional with your work**. It is easy to get carried away when you are presented with an opportunity and jump in with both feet without being aware of the pitfalls. For example, someone approaches you with a proposal for an exciting product that will automate customer onboarding and slash the time it takes by half. I have seen many people make a decision without checking what alternatives are available and if this is the optimal solution for them or not. They pay for the solution and end up not using it.

60. **Understand and address all four levels of planning**. You can use OKRs or a similar method to build a framework around the following levels:

   a) **Strategic:** This is the highest level of planning, meant to set the long- to mid-term goals of the organization and outline what needs to be done to reach them. It gives the organization direction and cascades to the tactical level of each function and department. Usually, it covers up to five years in advance, but it can be longer.

   b) **Enhancements:** This comes after the strategic level, where you identify projects and initiatives to reach the objectives. It includes developing KPIs, budgets, and departmental or functional planning.

c) Operational: Execution by the managers, frontline employees, and other staff. This level is about direct action on tasks, scheduling, admin, designing, and interviewing, to name just a few.

d) General: This is everything else that does not directly link to the goals but ensures that all projects and plans run smoothly. For example, employee performance bonuses are not directly linked to the organization's goal. However, they are crucial to keep everyone motivated and incentivized.

Dimension Five:

Founders

Dealing with founders can be tricky because they are all different. Each one will have their own experiences, personality, and motivations. It is critical that you ensure they remain focused on the big picture, respect the expertise of everyone on board, and make pragmatic, rather than emotional, decisions quickly when building and scaling the company. As a company leader, you are responsible for preventing founders from being caught unaware by their ego, biases, or other distractions.

If there is more than one founder, you will most likely report to just one of them. Being mindful of the power dynamics among the founders and the rest of the executive management and how you can fit is critical to your success in your role, especially if you're new in the company and have joined in the third or fourth year from the startup's inception.

61. Tame your ego. Your desire to win and be right all the time will most likely cause you to stop listening and push back against the founders, instead of educating them and listening to them. This could be fueled by their lack of experience if the founders are very young or they act superior to you because you work for them. Whatever the cause, you need to control your temptation to prove them wrong; instead, focus on the solution and direction. This means that if you're wrong, you should admit when you're wrong.

Rightfully, founders, as entrepreneurs, will likely be emotional about their work and the startup they're building. Sometimes, their pride will get in the way, and they will be sensitive to criticism. That is why you must be able to communicate feedback in a way that respects their feelings and achieves what is best for the company. This doesn't mean that you become a pushover. The first law of the *48 Laws of Power* is "never outshine the master." Making the founders appear more brilliant than they are could get you the support needed to achieve faster and better results for the company.[27]

62. Establish routine check-ins. It is easy to be consumed by your day-to-day tasks and problems and forget to keep your peers involved. When you start scaling the operation, it becomes even more important to synchronize with other function heads to avoid duplication of efforts and seize opportunities to fix any emerging challenges.

For example, you are working on a big project with a government entity in Morocco and they requested a set of features that will

---

27 Robert Greene and Joost Elffers, *The 48 Laws of Power*, concise ed (London: Profile books, 2002).

take lots of effort and money to develop and you're not sure if it's worth the time and effort. Ideally, you should consult with your commercial peers, to see if there are other customers within their network who might be interested in the same features. You could work with your country managers to facilitate a survey to help validate this information.

I like using team sports as an example from which to learn. The more a basketball team practices with each other and tries different strategies, the better harmonized and connected they become. The trust among them grows, and the coordination becomes a competitive advantage for the team. The same applies to the operation of a startup. The leadership team is usually small in number and is close in relationship. It is crucial that you all play in harmony and know when to pass the ball at the right time, parking your personal egos on the side and focusing on the greater good of the team and the success of your startup.

63. **Leading upward and horizontally, not only downward**.
Leading does not mean being bossy and telling people what to do. It's about taking the initiative and rallying people to contribute toward the company's objectives. You have to think from the business' perspective and avoid getting sucked into a narrow view in your call to action.

This also means that you must be good at navigating office politics. Being smart and delivering results isn't enough. Being loved by your team isn't enough. You have to understand the dynamics which build and sustain your power. You must maintain relationships and alliances with your founders and colleagues and build a visible brand that they all respect. As the executive coach Michael Wenderoth explains in his book *Get Promoted*, like a snowball getting larger as it rolls down a hill, the more you succeed, the more influence you have. Your influence will keep growing as the momentum builds, and your colleagues want to be associated with your success.[28] Many of us have survived the journey as CXOs in scale-ups, and have learned the hard way that there are always competing interests to navigate; meritocracy doesn't exist in absolute form.

Let's say that the company needs to hire some new customer service staff due to a sudden increase in clients, but there's a limit on new hires. You have approval to hire someone for a position in business development or finance, but you could live without that role for two to three months. Offer that position to customer service and take a step back to wait for the next available slot. Make sure that you are clear with the head of HR, CEO, and COO on why you are doing so and what you expect in return. Being a team player who acts as a partner does not mean you are a pushover and an easy target. Doing what is right for the company is your compass.

64. **Ensure alignment on vision, goals, and objectives**. Traditionally, we are taught that this is the responsibility of the CEO or COO and, in some cases, the head of human resources. However, it should be a collective responsibility of all leaders. When a CEO builds the startup leadership team, they will look for the expertise and leadership traits that fit their current and future needs.

---

28 Michael Wenderoth, *Get Promoted* (Unstoppable CEO Press, 2022), https://changwenderoth.com/book1/.

This happens by identifying and understanding the CEO's own strengths and weaknesses and filling in the skills and knowledge gaps by hiring the right subject matter experts or promoting emerging talents within the company—similar to what you would see in team sports like basketball, soccer, baseball, and cricket. The coach of a soccer team will assess the strengths and weaknesses of the existing team members, then they'll create a profile of the prospective members that they need to recruit to take the team to the next level. So if the soccer team is really strong on defense and weak at offense, the coach will hire great forwards who are quick, agile, and excellent at creating attack opportunities to score goals for the team.

The alignment of objectives happens when you follow a structured approach to building your OKRs by cascading them from the CEO to the CXOs and their teams, breaking down the vision and goals into objectives and key results to be achieved by projects and initiatives.

With some startup leaders, you might face resistance if you use jargon or academic terminologies, such as "design thinking," "OKRs," or "scrum." If that happens, avoid using such language, and instead work with them on a simplified process. If they add their own input into a document or a process, they'll have a sense of ownership and will be less resistant.

For example, instead of teaching teams how to use design thinking to improve a feature in your product, get them to interview a sample group of customers, and then build a prototype to solve the problem that you agreed on solving. This is a watered-down design thinking approach. As they work more on this project, they'll improve on it and become more engaged. Later when you provide them with design thinking training, they'll be more receptive to learning the methodology and applying what will improve their outcome.

65. **Build respectful relationships and remain neutral**. Be constructive when any of your colleagues are sharing their feedback, independent from their rank in the hierarchy, and avoid influencing them with your opinions and comments on their feedback, which could be perceived as you not listening or not appreciating their feedback. Instead, you could just say, "Thanks for sharing your feedback and observations. This is really helpful; please continue sharing them with me." The aim is to encourage them to do what's best for the business and to communicate anything that could contribute at improving the service delivery. It's important that you make the effort to spend time with colleagues outside the office, too, maybe over lunch or coffee. This way, you build trust and show appreciation for their contribution to your function or the company.

66. **Offer alternative perspectives to the CEO and other founders.** A common bias that founders have is hiring senior leaders who have personalities like them and the same thinking process. This is common especially at early stages of a startup's life and very common in single-founder startups. This will create and grow blind spots for the founders and the senior leadership in the form of setting the wrong priorities for projects toward building a scalable company. So your job is to make sure these biases are minimal and you always expand the perspective when assessing the right action for a specific time-sensitive problem.

For example, you have a vendor, a marketing agency, on retainer to support you with generating leads and you're the commercial head responsible for them. This agency is not delivering on what you're asking them to provide and keeps resisting following your approach: generating a specific number of leads that fit the quality you're looking for to have a healthy conversion rate of paying customers that help you achieve your targets. You escalate this issue to the Chief Commercial Officer (CCO) and the instinctive response is to replace this agency and do it immediately. However, you, as the commercial head who has a different view than the CCO, advise them to remain with them for a while, trying a new approach until you shortlist an alternative. If your personality was the same as the CCO, you would've fed into the CCO's emotion and caused a disruption in the business by firing the vendor too early without a succession plan for a new vendor, which would disrupt the operation and make you miss your target.

Dimension Six:

Investors

Whether you're interacting directly or indirectly with investors, it's crucial that you understand how they and their board representatives think, and what they expect. Most board members represent the current investors, and some might be hired to join as independent advisors due to their expertise. The CEO reports to the board, and the role of the board members is to use their experience to hold the company to account, guide the CEO's thinking to improve their critical decision-making, provide a nonbiased sanity check, and support transactional matters such as fundraising and mergers and acquisitions.[29] This will help you become more strategically synchronized with the CEO.

Let's say there's a major $200 million fundraising round, which means that the ownership percentage of the current investors will get diluted as new shares are issued to the new investors. The board will want

---

29 Brad Feld, Matt Blumberg, and Mahendra Ramsinghani, *Startup Boards: A Field Guide to Building and Leading an Effective Board of Directors*, Second edition (Hoboken, New Jersey: Wiley, 2022).

to make sure that the price per share increases by multiples of the original amount invested by each investor. In that case, you can align with the CEO and the board through hitting some key milestones that will support the new valuation. In most cases, you will probably not be dealing directly with the investors, but you might have some interaction with the board members who represent the investors. Even though your role is to support the CEO and not interact directly with the board, you still need to align on the deliverables, timelines, strategies, and progress. The following principles will help you do that.

67. **Help your CEO present the right data in the right way to the board**. Advise the CEO, where applicable, on the best way to present data requested by the board transparently and constructively, avoiding censoring bad news. If you're attending the board meetings with the CEO, you'll have a better view of how you can support them and get the most out of these meetings. Make sure the data is delivered on time and in the correct format.

68. **Align with the CEO on your strategic deliverables**. Having a strategic framework document helps you align with your CEO and peers on the direction of the company and how the future will look as you scale up operations. Typically, a strategic framework will cover the vision, mission, objectives, products, geographies, customer profiles, value delivery activities, and your competitive advantage. This document will also be shared with the board to ensure alignment of expectations.

Your and your peers' OKRs are extracted from and aligned with the strategic framework document, which will keep getting updated as you pivot and adjust your business model. Each key result is achieved through projects carried out by employees. If the strategic framework is aligned with the OKRs of the CEO, and these objectives are clearly communicated to staff, then employees will understand how their role and responsibilities contribute to the aims of the CEO and the success of the company. One approach to track this with more accuracy is implementing balanced score-cards, which could help you organize the efficiency tracking as the complexity driven by your growth increases.

69. **Avoid integrity pitfalls**. As the pressure to deliver targets and grow market share rises, so does the temptation to cut corners and fudge numbers. Your biases will kick in, and you'll start rationalizing bad decisions as good ones and making up excuses, blaming everyone and everything but yourself. Look for the signs and consult with your peers or line manager. The board members and audit committee are your safety net should such biased or emotional decisions be made. So make sure that you and your peers are proactive in introducing controls that prevent abuse of power by you or your colleagues. Companies that fail are usually blind to their biases.

70. **Respect and align with the audit committee and compensation committee**. The audit committee is critical for protecting leaders from making expensive mistakes that could bankrupt the company. Both audit and compensation committees

are required for startups planning an IPO. The audit committee ensures that there are controls in place to mitigate against all types of risks, and the compensation committee makes sure that staff are paid fairly and in line with industry averages.

71. **Act as a partner.** Part of your responsibility as a startup leader is to ensure stability during due diligence by investors and, if acquired, the integration management process. You must do your best to ensure that the focus remains on strategic alignment, cultural fit, and potential risks without being tempted to cover weaknesses or gaps. Every change, whether positive or negative, will face resistance from employees. So make sure you're prepared for it and that you're patient, firm, and fair.

Dimension Seven:

Community

It's easy to get lost in the weeds of running your business and not look at the bigger picture. When you're incredibly busy (when aren't you?!) or stressed, you can neglect your community. That's understandable, but you need to guard against it. Admittedly, you can't do everything at once, which is why knowing how to prioritize is so important, so you can keep moving forward step by step.

For example, when The Sims, the first example of a successful life simulation game that sold more than 200 million copies, was being built, it was just another emerging video game in its genre. However, as the designer Will Wright explained, understanding this particular ecosystem and engaging with the people in it is what led to the game's massive success.[30]

---

30 Will Wright, MASTERCLASS CLASS WITH WILL WRIGHT Game Design and Theory p, n.d., MasterClass.com.

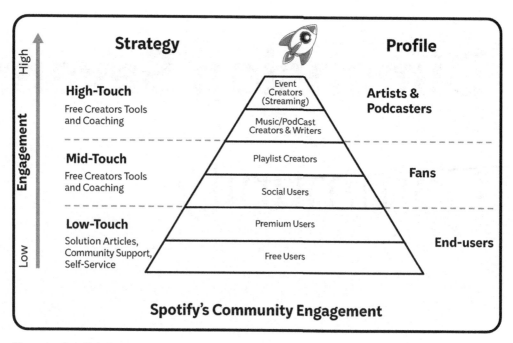

Figure 17: Spotify's Community Engagement

Another example would be how Spotify, the music streaming platform, built a community that helped it enhance its offering to its users in ways that no other platform, including Apple's Music, was able to achieve on that scale. Spotify follows a freemium pricing model, which brings with it lots of flexibility to the monetization process. This makes the onboarding friction of users very low. So, like YouTube, users can sign up and listen to music for free with limitations. Unless they upgrade to a premium version, they can't download the songs, skip songs, listen to all songs, or skip commercial ads. Most of their users are okay with the free version. So Spotify can still monetize them through selling ads. To keep growing the user base, Spotify realized early that they needed to create a community where their users are empowered based on their roles (or persona). The following is an abstract diagram that shows their level of engagement. The percentages are not real, and they're for illustration purposes.

Spotify's strategy was to use technology and the community to enable users to support themselves and concentrate its effort on the users who were willing to engage more with them and the customers. Spotify went the extra mile to the extent of creating tools and offering coaching to artists and podcasters to help them create more content on their platform.

In the beginning of the journey of building a community, you have to consider how the community partners see you. The community is made up of the following members, and each has their own needs and concerns to consider:

- investors;
- customers;
- employees;
- regulators; and
- fans and evangelists.

The following principles will help you understand their needs and how to engage with them as you scale your operation.

72. **Ensure all community groups are on your radar**. This will help you be more inclusive of all your user profiles and community members. This will help you avoid making mistakes that alienate and push your customers away from your company. Knowing your community will help you build your brand as you grow into a corporation. You can also align your activities with the local community to solve problems as part of your corporate social responsibility (CSR).

a) **Existing and potential customers:** As you evolve, creating unique engagement with your current customers will reward you with better positive word-of-mouth and will contribute to the reduction in churn, improvement to the customer lifetime value (LTV), and the improvement in popularity of your brand. Spotify was able to improve its offering by empowering customers to curate their experience and create custom playlists and to become more vocal fans of their artists through features like shared playlists—ideal for parties and social gatherings.

b) **Regulators (compliance):** If you are in a government sandbox or building a product in a regulated market, you must pay extra attention to how you are perceived and how your business contributes to the overall government objectives. In most startup ecosystems, the government proactively supports startups to succeed through eased regulatory constraints, grants, tax breaks, and access to government contracts as a supplier or a partner.

c) **Investors:** Aligning with the CEO will help keep the existing investors happy and attract new investors for your startup. This alignment is important even if you're not pitching to investors directly. The majority of investors know each other and prefer investing through syndicates, which helps them mitigate some of the risk associated with the due diligence process and as a socializing mechanism with other like-minded investors.

The more informed they are about what's happening in your industry and your startup's progress in capturing the target opportunity, the less challenging it will be to convince them to continue investing and help bring others to invest. Also, you have to keep in mind that investors like to brag about their successful investments. When your startup makes announcements and press releases of achievements and awards, your investors will most likely have a sense that they made a sound investment, especially if they hear it from their peers in the industry. Sometimes, you want to intentionally communicate a sense of urgency about investing in your startup by creating a fear-of-missing-out (FOMO) effect, which will give your investors the extra push they need to increase their support and make a decision to double down and invest money in the next rounds of funding and refer their peers and friends to join them in the investment. Depending on your role, you must understand how you can contribute to the bigger picture by aligning with the CEO, CFO, and other cofounders. In many cases, your role could be directly attending investor pitches and board meetings, or at other times, you could be just playing a support role to the CEO, cofounders, and CFO.

d) **Employees:** When positive word-of-mouth by your current and former employees travels out there in the market, the result will be increased employee retention and ease of attracting high-quality talent at competitive packages. It's not always about which startup pays the highest package. It's usually a combination of incentives, compensation, and a positive environment that cultivates learning, respect, and a moderate tolerance for mistakes. These qualities in a workplace create a sense of belonging and contribute to a strong company culture, which can get the employees, their families, and friends to talk positively about your startup, which will also reinforce the perceived value of working there among the employees.

e) **Industry:** To enable your company to innovate and grow faster, you could look at building an ecosystem around your company, like Apple Inc. They went from building products in a supply chain to providing a suite of digital services accessed by multiple devices, such as Apple Watch, Apple TV, MacBook, iPhone, and iPad, with one log-in account. Apple has become a channel for third-party applications like Netflix, Microsoft 365, and Evernote to have that same high-quality experience across all interfaces. This is a perfect example of building an ecosystemized business. An ecosystemized business is one that implements strategic partnerships to integrate the services, products, and business models to meet the user's needs while aligning the objectives and interests of the people working within the ecosystem.[31] The source of the ecosystem could be a blend of partnerships, mergers, or acquisitions.

f) **Partners and suppliers:** Ensuring that suppliers believe in you and want to work with you is very important. It will unlock certain advantages within your supply chain, such as

---

31 Julian Kawohl and Denis Krechting, *Ecosystemize Your Business: How to Succeed in the New Economy of Collaboration*, First printing edition (Erscheinungsort nicht ermittelbar: Ecosystemizer, 2022).

access to scarce resources or advantageous deals. You need to maintain a good relationship with them, especially with those that give you a competitive advantage or that you rely on greatly to keep you afloat. People prefer to work with people they like and trust.

g) **Educational institutions:** Universities can be a good source of talent and fresh ideas for startups. You need to be aware of what industry collaboration programs universities around you offer. Get involved with their internship programs when possible. Help them keep their curriculum up to date with the industry's future needs, which they'll appreciate and will unlock more value from the collaboration. Attracting and retaining the best talent, especially local nationals, is challenging in many startup ecosystems. You need the best talent to increase your chances of success and competitiveness. This will heighten the collective intelligence of the organization.

h) **Local community:** You need to ensure your community is not negatively impacted. It would be great if you could also benefit the community with your work and services. You notice that most software companies offer student discounts on their premium products. Some offer special pricing for senior citizens. Depending on the services and products you offer, there are ways to be creative in connecting with the community, such as raising funds for local charities by donating the revenues from some of the services during the fundraising campaign for the cause you're targeting. Toms (**www.toms.com**), the shoe manufacturing company, officially donates a third of its profits to community charity funds and activities.

73. **Use the right mix of communication channels**. Whether your communication channels are through email, social media, community forums, direct messaging, webinars, newsletters, blogs, applications, surveys and forms, or events, each group in your community has their preferred methods to receive information and updates. The challenge is to find the right blend of channels that work for the largest percentage of your target audience. To achieve that, you need to profile these audience segments by personas. Each persona is defined by many variables that include income, habits, culture, and education. At times, you might need to create your own channel through your platform or mobile application, if it makes sense for you.

74. Use the appropriate communication frequency and timing.

To increase the effectiveness of your digital communication with your audience, you have to be mindful of the best time to communicate with your target community member profiles and their preferences. For example, if you're sending educational newsletters, do you send them once a week on the weekend in the morning or send them out once a month on the first day of the week? There's no one right answer that fits all scenarios.

When you hire a marketing expert, they'll guide you through the norms of the region you're operating in and the habits of the target profiles and personas you're communicating with. To avoid falling into the trap of stereotyping and feeding your biases on what works and doesn't work, make sure you seek insights from marketing experts, previous campaign reports, and audience sample interviews, and that you experiment in a structured manner to find what gives the best results.

- If you run a weekly newsletter with a low opening rate, there could be multiple factors that caused this outcome, which include:

- The timing of the day or day of the week.

- The quality of the content might not be useful for the audience.

- The amount of information was overwhelming for their attention span.

The best way to find a better way is through following a disciplined routine of doing postmortems to assess the impact of each approach and changing one variable at a time. Sometimes, you just need consistency of weeks and months to build an audience.

There are many strategies to build a large community around your brand, as Spotify has done. You could call and interview a sample of your audience, which could give you some fresh ideas on the best time and frequency. Observe what your competitors are doing to gain some ideas and insights.

75. **Match your content to your audience**. Don't send everything to everyone. Be mindful of cultural sensitivities that might trigger certain issues or assumptions.

For example, if you own a fashion business and you want to run a campaign for your female customers in Saudi, you need to avoid using revealing images that might be acceptable in Europe or the US but could insult your target audience. It is about what is suitable for your customers.

76. **Collaborate with educational institutions**. Whether you are attending career day or conducting joint research and development, it is important to work with universities and colleges so you can access fresh ideas and bright young minds who could join your team and grow[32]. If students aspire to join your operation, word will spread about how great it is to work for your company, not just among their social circles (potential future employees) but among your existing staff too.

---

32 Moss Kanter, R. "A Four-Point Plan for Linking Innovation, Enterprises, and Jobs," *Harvard Business Review*, March 2012 n.d.

About the Author:

Adel is an experienced entrepreneur and operations expert who has developed a methodology called Skill Up as You Scale Up (SAUS) to give new leaders at startups the confidence and control to deliver results quickly. He has experience in international expansions, managing growth projects, and establishing regional offices. Adel has an educational background in corporate innovation and international business operations and focuses his research and publications on establishing operational excellence and innovation for startups and SMBs.

TO LEARN MORE ABOUT THE AUTHOR AND FOLLOW HIM:

ADEL8.COM
Skill-up As You Scale-up

Made in the USA
Columbia, SC
11 December 2024

49078400R00083